The New Americans
Recent Immigration and American Society

Edited by
Carola Suárez-Orozco and Marcelo Suárez-Orozco

A Series from LFB Scholarly

Immigrant Children
and the Politics of English-only
Views from the Classroom

Tom Stritikus

LFB Scholarly Publishing LLC
New York 2002

Library of Congress Cataloging-in-Publication Data

Stritikus, Tom.
  Immigrant children and the politics of English-only : views from the classroom / Tom Stritikus.
     p. cm. -- (The New Americans)
  Includes bibliographical references and index.
   ISBN 1-931202-28-1 (alk. paper)
   1. Immigrant children--Education--California--Case studies. 2. Hispanic Americans--Education--California--Case studies. 3. Education, Bilingual--California--Case studies. 4. English-only movement--California--Case studies. 5. Education, Bilingual--Government policy--California. 6. Education, Bilingual--Law and legislation--California. I. Title. II. New Americans (LFB Scholarly Publishing LLC)
  LC3732.C2 S82 2002
   371.826'91--dc21

2002004879

ISBN 1-931202-28-1

Printed on acid-free 250-year-life paper.

Manufactured in the United States of America.

Table of Contents

CHAPTER 6

CHAPTER 7

LIST OF TABLES

CHAPTER 1

Introduction

As typical teachers look at the students in their classrooms, they see dramatic differences from the classrooms of their youth. Today 1 in 3 children in the United States is from an ethnic or racially diverse group; 1 in 7 speaks a language other than English at home, and 1 in 15 is born outside the United States (Garcia, 1999). Linguistic and cultural diversity has become a reality in U.S. schools. Unfortunately, schools have fallen short in meeting the needs of diverse students (Suarez-Orozco & Suarez-Orozco, 1995). While one-tenth of European-American students leave high school without a diploma, one-fourth of African-American, one-third of Latino, and two-thirds of immigrant students drop out of school.

According to the 1990 U.S. Census, 6.3 million children in the United States spoke a language other than English at home. In 1997-1998, State Education Agencies reported that 7.8% (3, 452,875) of all U.S. schoolchildren were classified as Limited English Proficient (LEP). Since 1990, the growth rate for linguistically diverse students has hovered around 10%. While linguistic diversity is a reality throughout the United States, the highest populations are concentrated in select states. California, Texas, Florida, and New York enroll the largest numbers and largest percentage of students classified as LEP (Macias, 2000). In addition to these states, large populations of LEP students exist in the Southwestern states of Arizona, New Mexico, and Colorado. Macias (2000) reports that the greatest majority of LEP students report Spanish (78 %) as their primary language. Vietnamese (1.8 %), Hmong (1.6 %), Cantonese (1.1%), and Haitian Creole (1.1 %) make the up the other major native languages of students who are classified as LEP. Because the data for these figures was generated by reports from State Educational Agencies, these data are viewed as conservative estimates of the numbers of linguistically diverse students in the United States (Garcia, 1999; Macias, 2000).

From Demographics to School Decisions

Because linguistic and cultural diversity is a reality in the United States, schools and districts throughout the country are faced with the question of how to best educate this growing population of students. Central to these decisions is the role that the home language of students will play in instruction. Should students learn to read in their first language (L1) and then learn to read in their second language (L2)? Should recent immigrants be instructed in content area classes in their L1 so they do not fall behind in the critical areas of math, science, and social studies? Or, will cultural and linguistically diverse students benefit from instruction provided solely in English? Across the nation, schools and districts struggle with these questions.

A variety of instructional programs have been devised and implemented over the last several decades to attempt to meet the educational needs of the significant population of linguistically diverse students. Various program models differ in the role that students' L1 plays in instruction. In an attempt to understand the architecture of programs districts and schools have designed and implemented for students, I present the six major program types identified by August and Hakuta's (1997) comprehensive review of the research regarding linguistic minority students:

> **Submersion**: Students are placed in regular English-only classrooms and are given no special instructional support. (This approach is illegal in the U.S. as a result of Supreme Court decision in *Lau v. Nichols*. The Court did not prescribe a specific remedy but requires a program appropriate to the needs of English language learners.)

English as a Second Language (ESL): No instruction in a student's primary language; ESL is taught either through pullout programs or is integrated with academic content throughout the day.

Structured Immersion: Instruction conducted in English to a classroom of English-language learners. An attempt is made to adjust the level of English so that subject matter is comprehensible.

Transitional Bilingual Education (TBE): Students receive some degree of instruction in their primary language for a period of time; however, the goal of the program is transition to English-only instruction as rapidly as possible, generally within 1-3 years.

Maintenance Bilingual Education (MBE): Students receive instruction in their primary language and in English throughout the elementary school years (K-6) with the goal of developing academic proficiency in both languages.

Two-Way Developmental Bilingual Programs: Language majority and language minority students are instructed together in the same program with the goal of each group achieving bilingualism and biliteracy.

The six programs identified here are not an exhaustive list. Additionally, these programs do not exist in pure forms. Schools and districts use combinations and permutations of these programs to attempt to meet the needs of their students.

A variety of large and small-scale studies have examined the effectiveness of these programs. The researchers of the studies have willingly and unwillingly become a part of the great debate about the effectiveness of bilingual education. In order to get a sense of the existing research and the way it has been positioned in policy debates, I review a few of the seminal studies examining the effectiveness of various program types.

The Bilingual Debate and the Research Context

As bilingual education continued to the evolve throughout the 1960s
and 1970s, there was a major split in public opinion regarding the
program. Colin Baker (2001) explains that one branch of public opinion
saw bilingual education as failing to foster social integration and a
waste of public funds. By many opponents of bilingual education,
Latinos and supporters of bilingual education were portrayed as
employing bilingual education for their own political gain (Baker,
2001).   Bilingual education is not, and never has been, a neutral
process. The education of linguistically diverse students is situated in
larger issues about immigration, distribution of wealth and power, and
the empowerment of students (Cummins, 1996; 2000; Heller, 1994).
Critics of bilingual education have drawn from two major studies to
attempt to move schools and districts away from using bilingual
education. Both of these studies were reviews of existing research.

One study which was used in the early 1980s to justify an
English-only approach is the work of Keith Baker and Adriana de
Kanter (1983). They conducted a major review of transitional
bilingual programs in a study commissioned by the United States
Federal Government. They reviewed "methodologically acceptable"
studies on bilingual education programs with the specific intent to see
if transitional bilingual education was more effective than other
programs which made no use of L1. They concluded that the belief
that children should be taught in a language they understand did not
preclude success in English-only instructional situations. The review
supported the use of English-only instruction arguing that in the
American context there was little inherent value in students'
development of bilingualism.

Several scholars have pointed out methodological concerns with
the Baker and de Kanter (1983) review. Colin Baker (2001) points out
that the study had "a narrow range of expected outcomes for bilingual
education in the [research] questions. Only English language, and
non-language subject areas were considered as the desirable outcome
of schooling. Other outcomes such as self-esteem, employment,
preservation of minority languages, and the value of different cultures
were not considered" (p. 246). Stritikus and Manyak (2000) argue
that the techniques used to determine which of the 300 studies were
methodologically acceptable were plagued with inappropriate and

misleading labeling of programs. Despite these methodological flaws, the Baker and de Kanter (1983) review has been used as justification for the preferences towards English-only and transitional programs in many districts and schools.

Similar methodological concerns have been raised about the second major review of research which has been used to justify the use of English-only instruction. Rossel and Baker (1996) reviewed 72 "methodologically acceptable" studies. Based on their review, they concluded that structured immersion was the best program for linguistically diverse students, particularly in the area of reading achievement. The study is widely cited by critics of bilingual education. Several researchers have noted that the review is also plagued by many of the same methodological issues as Baker and de Kanter (1983). In particular, the Rossel and Baker (1996) review applied arbitrary and inconsistent criteria to establish methodologically acceptable studies, and inaccurate and arbitrary labeling of programs (Cummins, 1999; Stritikus & Manyak, 2000).

Research Base Supporting Bilingual Education

As critics of bilingual education have drawn heavily from the work of Rossel and Baker (1996) and Baker and de Kanter (1983) to push educational policy, advocates of bilingual education have drawn from a body of research which has reached opposite conclusions and supports the use of students' native language in instruction. Willig (1985) conducted a meta-analysis of 23 of the 28 studies reviewed by Baker and de Kanter (1983). Meta-analysis is a collection of systematic techniques for resolving apparent contradictions in research findings. Meta-analysis translates results from different studies to a common metric and statistically explores relationships between study characteristics and findings (Glass, McGaw, & Smith, 1981). Employing this technique, Willig (1985) found small to moderate effects in favor of bilingual education. Additionally, Willig (1985) concluded that when studies were well designed, they tended to show the benefits of bilingual education.

Many of the evaluation studies have conducted relatively short-term assessments of children in bilingual and English-only programs, measuring achievement over a one- to two-year period. This approach appears particularly dubious in light of the limited longitudinal data available on the achievement of English-language learners. The strengths of a long-term approach to the effectiveness question has been established by Ramirez (1992) and Thomas and Colliers (1997). Specifically, Ramirez (1992) found important differences in the growth curves of children in immersion, transitional bilingual education (TBE), and maintenance bilingual education (MBE) programs during the later elementary grades that favored the children in MBE programs. Similarly, preliminary findings from a study-in-progress analyzing achievement data from a series of 3-6 year longitudinal studies involving 24,000 language minority students indicates that children in two-way developmental bilingual and MBE programs experience a sharp increase in English-language achievement after five to seven years of schooling (Thomas & Collier, 1997). These data suggest that children in certain bilingual programs may make significant gains in English-language achievement toward the end of elementary school – gains that are undetected by program evaluations focused on short-term achievement.

Beyond Research on Program Types

For policy-makers, state and district decision-makers, and teachers, research examining the success or failure of various program types has not completely addressed the central question of how best to educate culturally and linguistically diverse students. Fortunately, a body of research has reported detailed studies of what has worked in actual classrooms. Rather than focus on program models, this body of research has concentrated on the characteristics of schools and classrooms which contribute to successful educational practice for culturally and linguistically diverse students.

August and Hakuta (1997) provide a comprehensive review of optimal learning conditions which serve linguistically and culturally diverse student populations—conditions leading to high academic performance. Their review of some 33 studies indicates there is a set of generally agreed upon practices which foster academic success. It is important to note, that these practices can exist across program types. August and Hukuta (1997) report found that the following school and classroom characteristics were likely to lead to academic success:

A supportive school-wide climate, school leadership, a customized learning environment, articulation and coordination within and between schools, use of native language and culture in instruction, a balanced curriculum that includes both basic and higher-order skills, explicit skill instruction, opportunities for student-directed instruction, use of instructional strategies that enhance understanding, opportunities for practice, systematic student assessment, staff development, and home and parent involvement. (August & Hakuta, 1997, p. 171)

Thus, culturally and linguistically diverse students can benefit greatly from cognitively challenging and student-centered instruction which makes use of cultural and linguistic resources of students.

Proposition 227: The Attempt to End Bilingual Education

In the summer of 1997, the bilingual education debate moved from the pages of academic journals and the proceedings of federal and district educational agencies to the center of a public controversy about the education of culturally and linguistically diverse students. Ron Unz, a former Republican gubernatorial candidate and millionaire software developer, launched "English for the Children," an initiative designed to end bilingual education programs in the state of California. Through the initiative process voters can take political and legal processes directly into their own hands by proposing changes to state laws.

In the campaign against bilingual education, Ron Unz leveraged a considerable amount of his personal fortune to attempt to persuade California voters to support his initiative. Much of his media efforts were directed at discrediting and demeaning the scholarly work regarding the effectiveness of bilingual education. Ron Unz attempted to cast the restriction of native language instruction in terms of a benevolent pro-immigrant stance. Arguing that he represented the true will of immigrants across California, Unz maintained that he was merely assisting Latinos and other recent immigrants free themselves from bilingual education (Riccardi, 1997).

Although Unz attempted to maintain a "pro-immigrant" stance, the campaign proved to be very racially divisive. Inevitably, much of the public discourse supporting the passage of Proposition 227 took nativist and xenophobic positions (Kerper-Mora, 2000; Orellana et al., 1999). California became the center of a national debate between "nativist" and "multiculturalist" visions of education. The nativist position represented by Proposition 227 assumed a benevolent view of Americanization and the role that rapid learning of English plays in the process (Kerper-Mora, 2000).

Despite being opposed by many major political figures in California, President Clinton, and nearly all state-wide teaching and educational associations, in June of 1998 Proposition 227 passed by a majority of 61% percent of the vote. Once passed by the voting public, the initiative immediately became law and districts were given 60 days to be in full compliance with its provisions. The law requires that "all children in California public schools be taught English by being taught in English" (California Education Code, Chapter 3, Article I. Section 305). Under the law, English language learner (ELL) students who do not have sufficient English development to manage in a mainstream classroom are eligible to receive one year of structured English immersion (SEI)—a program of English instruction not described in detail in the law except to require that instruction be "nearly all" in English.

The passage of Proposition 227 marked a significant event in California's educational history. Never before had the voting public been asked to vote on a specific educational strategy. Curriculum and programmatic decisions for students have generally been the responsibility of the education community. Gándara, et al., (2000) argue that because Proposition 227 attempted to take decision-making power away from the educational community, the law was opposed by every major educational association in the state.

The law represents the latest policy move in a long and often contentious debate surrounding bilingual education. California, one of the first states to enact a comprehensive bilingual education bill, has been at the center of that debate. Following the historic *Lau vs. Nichols* (1974) Supreme Court decision requiring schools to take affirmative steps to ensure the meaningful participation of English learners, the Chacon-Moscone Bilingual-Bicultural Act of 1976 was passed. It declared "that the primary goal of all programs under this article [was], as effectively and efficiently as possible, to develop in each child fluency in English" (California Education Code, 1976, Section 52161), while at the same time ensuring that they had access to the core curriculum. The law specified that the preferred manner for doing so was primary language instruction.

Proposition 227 directly challenged and attempted to end primary language instruction. The new law requires that after one year of "sheltered English immersion" (SEI), children are expected to integrate into mainstream English classrooms, where instruction is required to be "overwhelmingly" in English. If parents or legal guardians find that District or school personnel, including classroom teachers, "willfully and repeatedly refuse" to provide the English instruction as required, they have the right to sue for damages. Thus, in order to avoid legal liability it was necessary for teachers and district personnel to understand and to implement the law fully. Given the ambiguity of many of the law's provisions, the threat of legal sanction created a great sense of insecurity with many district and school personnel across the state (Stritikus & Garcia, 2000).

The only legal alternative to SEI and/or mainstream English classrooms is the parental waiver process. According to the new law, children who have special language needs, or whose parents specifically request it, can be placed in "Alternative Programs," most likely some form of bilingual program that includes instruction in the child's primary language. In order for a child to be enrolled in an Alternative Program, the parent or guardian must annually visit the school and sign a waiver requesting the placement. The first year a child enters California schools, however, she must go through 30 days of "observation," generally conducted in English language classrooms, regardless of the signed waiver. Once the 30 days is completed, the child can enroll in an Alternative Program.

Despite its attempt to prescribe a uniform solution for the education of linguistically and culturally diverse students across the state, the law's impact on educational services for language minority students has varied widely from district to district, school to school, and, in some cases, classroom to classroom. Garcia & Curry-Rodriguez (2000) report that some districts across the state have used the waiver clause of the law to pursue district-wide waivers; others have implemented the English-only provisions of the law; and a third group has left the primary decisions up to individual schools. Districts with longstanding bilingual programs were more likely to pursue parental waivers in order to maintain their existing programs than were districts with weaker primary language programs (Gándara, et al., 2000; Garcia & Curry-Rodriguez, 2000).

The influence that Proposition 227 will ultimately have on educational programs for linguistically and culturally diverse students is still contested. As attorneys, policy makers, and advocates of primary language instruction and English-only approaches attempt to shape the nature of the law, teachers and students face its reality on a daily basis.

Proposition 227 and Language Ideology

By imposing the view that learning English as quickly as possible is essential for immigrant students, Proposition 227 positions all other languages as having a marginal status. By attempting to dictate language use in the classroom, the law enacted an ideology of monolingualism (Schmidt, 2000; Tollefson, 1995).

The nativist position advanced by Proposition 227 is contrasted by multiculturalist and mutilingualist notions that English-only instruction is deeply problematic. Rather than view the home language and culture through a lens of deficit, multiculturalist and multilinguilist perspectives urge schools to see these as valuable educational resources. (Banks, 1995; Garcia, 1999; Gutiérrez, et al., 2000; Olneck, 1995). Proposition 227 presents a direct challenge to the notion that languages other than English have a legitimate and valuable place in the education of diverse students. Hence, the normative assumptions underlying Proposition 227 position the language and culture of diverse students in a subordinate and inferior role to English (Auerbach, 1995; Cummins, 2000; Kerper-Mora, 2000).

These normative assumptions have important consequence that extend beyond the classroom. The nature of the law works to position certain groups in a peripheral role in American society. Sekhon (1999), in an article assessing the legal and political implications of the proposition, argues that Proposition 227 positions immigrants on the outside of mainstream America:

> Proposition 227 positions English as "our" language by constructing it as our unlearned capacity: It is our birthright. The proposition differentiates "us" from "them" by denominating them in terms of an essential inability to call English their own. They must learn it. Proposition 227 not

only demands that they learn out language, it demands that they forget their own. In so demanding, the proposition not only unleashes a salvo in the bilingual education debate, but is a moment in the broader debate over assimilation and acculturation. (p. 1445)

Thus, in its scope, focus, and ideological implications, Proposition 227 differs markedly from past educational reforms. Teachers were not only asked to shift educational practice, but asked to participate in new ways in the American project of racialization (Olsen, 1997). Since working to pass Proposition 227 in California, Unz has exported his campaign against bilingual education to other states, including passing an even more restrictive initiative in Arizona. The movement to end bilingual education has now become part of a national debate about the legitimacy of languages other than English in school settings.

In attempt to understand how this debate is shaping the lives of teachers and students, I present the case of one district's experience with the changes brought about by Proposition 227. The decisions made by the district represent how competing ideologies regarding bilingual education and immigrant students surface in the daily practice of schools. By closely examining how Proposition 227 plays out in the lives of four teachers in the district, I seek to contribute to our understanding of how the recent spate of anti-bilingual initiatives is influencing the lives of students and teachers. Schools and districts across the nation grapple with the questions that Proposition 227 brought to the surface. By examining how one district dealt with these questions, I hope we can learn from their mistakes and benefit from their successes.

CHAPTER 2

Teachers' Place in the Local Enactment of Language Policy

I can't be optimistic about our program because we're not letting the kids absorb the language. They're [administration and Open Court Literacy Coaches] moving them too fast. They're not taking into consideration that these kids need time to learn the language. I think 227 could work if the wrong people don't get a hold of it.

(Celia, 1st grade teacher, Westway Elementary)

I feel the best thing to do is educate these children in English. I come from a family where my parents were in the exact same boat as adults. So, I understand how it is to feel clueless to everything. But my own personal beliefs about living in this country are that the best thing to do is to give them as much English and educate them so that they can get higher level types of jobs.

(Connie, 3rd grade teacher, Westway Elementary)

I am a bilingual teacher because I believe in bilingual education. I believe everybody has the right to speak their own language, and I believe that if America is a free country then nobody should deny you the right to get an education in your first language. These children are going to be our future

leaders in a few years. What kind of children do you want to make?
(Angelica, 2nd grade bilingual teacher, Open Valley Elementary)

How do they [Proposition 227 supporters] think the students are going to communicate with their grandparents in Mexico. It's like, yes, we [bilingual teachers] obviously know they need English for a better career and to have a better future, but what about their relationships with their family and culture?
(Elisa, 3rd grade bilingual teacher, Open Valley Elementary)

Cautious optimism, unconditional acceptance, and opposition were the feelings and perceptions these four teachers had towards Proposition 227. Each of these teachers' opinions of the law belied something about their professional identities: their personal life experiences, their views about culture and language, and their perception of what it meant to "be American." While each of these teachers had well defined and deeply held beliefs about the new law's influence on their classrooms and their students, the personal views of teachers have seldom been considered a serious point of study in the implementation of policy. Policy research has been dominated by "input-output" analysis that has viewed talking to teachers as an irrelevant method for illuminating the effects of policy (Darling-Hammond, 1990). This examination of Proposition 227 implementation begins with the idea that the beliefs and perceptions of teachers play a large role in teachers' negotiations of the policy context created by Proposition 227.

This study examines the local enactment of policy in classroom literacy contexts against teachers' individual qualities. The purpose of this study is to understand how Proposition 227 influences the nature of teachers' work in and out of classrooms; and how teachers, through that work, influence the nature of Proposition 227 as reform strategy.

Research Questions and Purpose of the Study

The primary aim of this research is to understand the nature of teachers' work in and out of classroom literacy contexts in the new policy environment created by Proposition 227. The study focuses on the manner in which teachers negotiate the demands of Proposition 227 implementation decisions. I consider several factors that contribute to the connection between policy and practice. I examine the local enactment of policy by tracing teachers' experiences of district and school decisions regarding Proposition 227 implementation.

To explore the connections between policy and practice, I utilized the ethnographic method to study literacy instruction in two schools. Both schools were in "Walton Unified School District," [1] a rural district that gave individual schools authority to determine their own Proposition 227 implementation plans. In the first year of Proposition 227, one school, "Open Valley," made the school-wide decision to maintain the school's primary language program through parental waivers. Open Valley teachers organized meetings in which they informed parents about waivers and used school testing data to convince parents to save the primary language program at the school. At "Westway Elementary," the principal made the decision not to pursue waivers, so the bilingual program at the school was eliminated. During the second year of Proposition 227, both schools kept the same instructional arrangements they established during the first year of implementation. Open Valley became a Charter School to free itself from having to collect the waivers each year. Westway continued its practice of placing all English language learner students in English-only classrooms.

By focusing on the teachers' negotiation of literacy instruction, this study examines classroom practice against a backdrop of school-wide, district-wide, and statewide issues as they pertain to the implementation of Proposition 227. This research connects teacher perceptions about Proposition 227 and its implementation with day-to-day literacy practices. I examine both policy- and practice-based questions as I explore the connections among statewide policy, district and school decisions, the individual characteristics of teachers, and classroom practice. The research is guided by the following questions:

Overarching Questions

How does Proposition 227 as a reform influence the nature of teachers' work in and out of classroom literacy contexts?

---

[1] To protect the confidentiality of the research participants, all names of people, schools, and districts in this book are pseudonyms.

How does teachers' work influence the nature of Proposition 227 as a reform strategy?

Policy Questions (Chapter 4)

How do decisions made at the district and school level in regards to Proposition 227 allow or impede certain types of teacher agency? How is that local agency mediated by organizational structures within districts/schools?

Practice Question (Chapters 5 & 6)

What is the relationship between teachers' individual qualities and the contexts in which they work and their implementation and negotiation of literacy instruction?

The research questions guiding this project are grounded in certain assumptions about the nature of policy- and practice-based issues as they relate to the literacy instruction of linguistically and culturally diverse students. The theoretical framework guiding this investigation of the local enactment of policy is addressed in the following section.

THEORETICAL BACKGROUND

This study attempts to understand the connection between policy and practice as they relate to the implementation of Proposition 227 in a rural California school district. To do so, this study utilizes policy research to understand teachers' roles in top-down reform situations. A great deal has been written about the types of educational reform strategies that are likely to succeed and the types that are likely to fail. By examining this body of research with an eye on Proposition 227 implementation, I hope to develop a clear understanding of the role of teachers in the reform and policy implementation process. To give clarity to issues of instructional practice as they relate to my study, I will borrow from educational research based on sociocultural perspectives. Such research is one way to approach issues of context, practice, and literacy as they relate to Proposition 227 implementation.

Proposition 227 and Teachers' Roles in the Reform Process

California's Proposition 227 has placed the state's educational system on uncharted ground. Not only is the source of the reform—the voting public—unique for educational change, but the scope of changes the new law mandates has not been seen since the desegregation decisions of the 1950s. While Proposition 227 might not be the type of reform that scholars of school "restructuring" have written about and advocated (e.g., Darling-Hammond, 1993; McLaughlin, 1989; Sizer, 1984), much of the research literature on school reform is relevant in analyzing how Proposition 227 is taking shape and affecting teachers and students. By looking at the factors that have contributed to the success or failure of reform attempts, a perspective can be built that begins to account for the role that teachers play in the process.

Various scholars have traced reform attempts taking particular perspectives about the best ways to change schools and school practice. From approaches that stressed increased bureaucratization and control mechanisms of teachers (McNeil, 1986), to attempts that stressed "commitment strategies" and attempt to get teachers to "buy-into" reform agendas (Rowan, 1990), many of these perspectives saw teachers as a generic group to be controlled. After these views of reform came "restructuring" attempts, which assumed that by making fundamental changes to school structure, changes in instruction and practice would occur (Elmore, 1995; Lieberman, 1995). Although educational policy research has come closer to examining teachers' roles in the reform process, reform has generally been viewed as something done *to* or *for* the teacher (Fullan, 1991; and Fullan & Hargreaves, 1992). Even Fullan (1991) and Hargreaves (1994), who tend to take a more active view of teachers' roles in the reform process, tend to frame teachers as a group, not as individuals whose unique characteristics will impact the shape of reform.

These waves of reform study and advocacy presented only partial pictures of the ways educational reforms are enacted, mediated, and shaped in the classroom. The field's inability to account completely for the nature and nuances of reform implementation stems from the conception of teachers' roles in the process. When reform attempts found their way to classrooms, teachers were far more dynamic participants than advocates and scholars of restructuring had envisioned (Woods, 1994). It is for this reason that this attempt to understand policy- and practice-based questions will incorporate teachers' perspectives about their schools' implementations of Proposition 227.

In order to fully understand how the individual characteristics of teachers might impact the implementation of Proposition 227, a theoretical frame in which teachers are seen as unique and active individuals must be built. A perspective that teachers are more than a collective and generic group in the reform process emerged in work examining England's 1988 National Curriculum Initiative. Osborn and Broadfoot (1992) and Woods (1994) adopt a dynamic conception of the reform process and view the National Curriculum Initiative as a site of struggle. Rather than focus on teachers as a generic whole, they argue that new policy decisions must be mediated through and by teachers: "The way that teachers translate new initiatives into practice are dependent upon their prior beliefs and practices" (Vulliamy & Webb, 1993, p. 21). Woods examined specific ways that teachers' biographies and their reasons for entry into the profession would cause them to resist or appropriate particular reforms. Teachers who resisted the National Curriculum had a clearly defined idea of what the needs of their students were—needs they felt were not being addressed by the proposed changes. The particular school studied by Woods was a low-performing high-poverty school that served immigrant children. From their past experiences in working with their students, the resisting teachers concluded that the National Curriculum offered them nothing new and rejected the order on ideological grounds. Woods contends that when teachers' ideological conflict is not severe, teachers appropriate elements of the reform into their pre-existing practices.

Two extremely important points came out of Woods' research on the National Curriculum that are directly related to understanding teacher reaction to Proposition 227. First, Woods puts a new spin on ideas presented by Lortie (1975), who claims that the lack of distinct teacher socialization process causes teachers to retreat to what they learned through their experiences as students. In short, teachers teach how they were taught. While this analysis might describe some teacher practice, its overly deterministic view of the way classroom practice is shaped prevents an understanding of teachers as active individuals. Woods (1994) claims that teachers who resisted aspects of the National Curriculum were reacting—not retreating—to their past experiences as students. Having been bored and marginalized by traditional approaches as students, the teachers in the study made conscious decisions not to implement the reforms in their classrooms. Thus, examinations of teachers' educational biographies are crucial to understand the reality of teachers' reaction to reform attempts.

A second perspective expanded by the Woods (1994) study is the role of collaboration in teacher reaction to reform. Teachers in the study that demonstrated resistance to reforms were aided by work environments with like-minded colleagues. Parents, administrators, and teachers formed a power base from which to respond to top-down reforms. Similarly, Nias (1989) argues that teachers "self-protect" by interacting with like-minded colleagues. Consequently, an examination of the organizational context in which teachers work will be an essential part of understanding teacher reaction to Proposition 227.

Arguing against seeing the teacher as merely a "conductor" of policy mandates, Darling-Hammond (1990) contends that to make policy studies come alive, teachers' instructional choices must be examined against both the policy context and their beliefs and ideologies. Building from a perspective that puts the teacher in the center of policy studies, Jennings (1996), examining policy and practice connections of reading reforms in Michigan, argues that understanding policy requires viewing teacher beliefs about policy against a background of practice. Cohen and Ball (1990) similarly argue that teachers enact new instructional policy in light of inherited knowledge, beliefs, and past practices. These perspectives of teachers' roles in the reform process dispute the claim that state and district policy homogenize school experience.

This review of the research literature on educational reform demonstrates that to understand policy as it relates to educational practice, we must move away from one-dimensional views of teachers. The research of Jennings (1996), Darling-Hammond (1990), Cohen and Ball (1990), Osborn and Broadfoot (1992), and Woods (1994) make a clear case that talking to teachers is not an irrelevant part of policy research. By examining educational policy implementation through the eyes of teachers, I hope to offer a rich account of Proposition 227's influence on teachers' work in and out of the classroom.

Sociocultural Perspectives on Context, Practice, and Literacy

While a significant part of this study is an attempt to understand how teacher ideology is being shaped by and shaping the nature of

Proposition 227 implementation, equally important is understanding the nature of literacy instruction in the contexts created by Proposition 227. Accomplishing this task requires drawing from theoretical perspectives that illuminate terms such as context, practice, and literacy.

Research in the area of second language development has long considered the importance of contextual factors in student learning. Wong Fillmore (1992) argues that the situation and interactional context in which language development takes places is the single most important issue as to whether successful language and literacy development will occur. The notion of the learning situation as merely existing in the physical space of the classroom has come to be viewed as an inadequate way to understand the complexities of the classroom. Garcia (1999) argues that learning situations of immigrant students are best understood as places where student learning and development are considered in light of their past and present linguistic, sociocultural and cognitive interactions with home and community environments.

In this sense, context becomes more than the physical setting of instruction. Context is the sum total of interactional factors between teachers and students. Viewing classrooms with this lens creates an imperative to understand how learning is connected to contextual issues. Diaz, Moll, and Mehan (1986) explain:

> Hence, in the study of any learning activity, the unit of analysis becomes the activity, the unit of analysis becomes the act or system of acts by which learning is composed, as seen in the context of the classroom, the school, and the community. Consequently, a critical task in the analysis of educational interactions becomes the careful and detailed description of the learning activity and its constituent sequence of acts. (p. 192)

Focusing on the interactional factors, Diaz, et al., (1986) examine the situations in which reading instruction occurs. They conclude that the social organization of the reading lesson—the interaction between student and teacher—drastically changed the nature of the learning situation. It was through an analysis of the interactional nature of the learning event that Diaz, et al. (1986) were able to consider ways teachers might better be able to reconstruct and change the learning context to the benefit of students.

This study will attempt to make sense of context as it relates to reading instruction. During my observations, I paid close attention to how interactional structures created opportunities for success or failure of student literacy development. Although I did not intend to impose a definition of literacy upon the classes I observed, I did enter the field with certain ideas about the nature of literacy and how literacy connects to—and in some cases creates—contexts. Dyson (1993) argues that literacy is a cultural tool for taking action in the world whose power comes from its ability to connect to others across time, and to organize thoughts, feelings and experience. In this sociocultural conception of literacy, negotiation and interaction amongst participants in the learning situation are key factors in shaping the nature of literacy instruction.

Because I seek to examine practice in the face of policy changes, I advance a definition of practice which attempts to connect issues of conceptions of literacy with the importance of context in educational situations. Hanks (1992) argues that practice is the place that formal and relational aspects of language meet as the sum total of form, activity, and ideology. To understand practice, Hanks argues that human activity and the formal structures in which practice occurs can not be separated from the ideological dimensions of language use and human interaction.

I start with the belief that understanding a particular educational policy requires building a clear picture of teachers' ideological reaction to that policy. Teachers' reactions to that policy must be understood as occurring in contexts created by actions at the state, district, and school-site level. Seeing classroom contexts and instructional practice as closely related to ideology places the classroom as one of the key places to examine instruction in light of particular policy changes.

Plan for the Book

In chapter 3, I provide a methodological description of my procedures used in gaining entry to the school sites, my criteria for selecting focal teachers and focal classroom events, my data collection procedure, and my process for data analysis. In addition, I provide a description of the research sites.

In Chapter 4, I consider the role that the individual qualities of the teachers—including their entry into the field, their beliefs about the culture and language of their students, and their ideological response to

Proposition 227—played in the negotiation of policy at the local level. I detail the Proposition 227 implementation decisions at the district and school level, and consider how these decisions allowed or impeded certain types of agency for the teachers.

In Chapters 5 and 6, I examine practice-based issues in the four classrooms of the four focal teachers of this research. Having established in Chapter 4 that teachers are not just conduits of policy, I look at the varied manifestations of the local enactment of policy. I address the connection between teachers' individual qualities and contexts for literacy instruction in their classrooms. My intent in examining detailed examples of classroom life is to provide a textured account of the how teachers negotiated the demands of Proposition 227 as a reform effort.

In Chapter 7, I focus on the significance of the findings for the understanding of language policy and the education of culturally and linguistically diverse students.

CHAPTER 3

Research Methods, Research Site and Participants

In this chapter, I describe the research methodology guiding data collection and data analysis for this research project. I begin with an explanation and justification of my use of the ethnographic method. I then describe the research site by detailing relevant information about the district, schools, and four teachers who were the focus of study in this research. I conclude with a detailed description of the procedures I used during data collection and data analysis.

ETHNOGRAPHY: THROUGH THE EYES OF THE TEACHER

In this section I discuss my orientation to and use of the ethnographic method that guided data collection procedures and analysis of this project. Because my major purpose was to see Proposition 227 through the eyes of teachers, I used ethnography because it was one of the best ways to understand what it meant to be a teacher in the post-

Proposition 227 policy context. The use of the ethnographic method in educational research has long exposed salient factors of classroom life (Erickson, 1986). Although ethnography has illuminated the cultural understandings of the participants in educational situations, its place in educational policy research has been marginal. Positivist approaches relying on input-output models have dominated discussions of educational policy. Such models involve documenting the basic elements of policy and measuring the effects, usually quantitatively, with reference to students' standardized achievement test scores. Input-output models do not examine how policy recipients at various levels, including teachers, students, and administrators, experience, understand and attempt to incorporate the intended policies (Darling-Hammond, 1990). Consequently, we are left without useful explanations for how policy is lived and adopted, or not adopted, in local settings. Research in the area of bilingualism and second language development has focused on evaluation, instructional strategies, and second language development theory (August & Hakuta, 1997). While these are all valuable endeavors, they, too, provide a limited picture of the local enactment of policy.

Both the place of teachers in policy research and the nature of research on bilingualism led me to believe that this investigation of policy to practice would best be conducted using an ethnographic approach. My hope was that focusing on the situated nature of the local enactment of policy would expose elements of Proposition 227 implementation that traditional research approaches might not expose.

As a research method, ethnography attempts to uncover the way members of a particular community experience life in that community. In the study of a school or classroom, ethnography focuses on how the members of the school community—administrators, teachers, and students—understand membership and the rules of participation of that community. Deal (1985) claims that ethnographers attempt to define culture by asking "What does it mean to be a member of this group?" and "What is going on here? How does this work?" Such questions eventually lead the researcher to be able to answer questions related to the "way things are done around here."

While I entered the field with certain ideas or images (Becker, 1998) about policy, teaching, and Proposition 227, my primary purpose was to build an understanding of how the teachers who participated in this study saw and experienced the new policy context.

To do so meant my research needed to be situated in the work lives of the teachers. My observations focused on developing insight into how the teachers saw the world. This required developing an emic perspective as explained in Green, Dixon, & Zaharlick (in press):

> Ethnographers seek understandings of the cultural patterns and practices of everyday life of the group under study from an emic or insider's perspective. Through an interactive and responsive process that is recursive in nature, the ethnographer examines what members need to know to produce, understand, and predict in order to participate as a member of the group. (Green, et al., in press).

Such a perspective requires focusing on culture not as a static entity experienced by members, but as a set of "imperfectly laid out principles" (Spradely, 1980, p. 9) that create a set of practices members experience and influence. Green et al. (in press) conclude, "Therefore culture is not a variable or even a set of variables, but a set of practices and principles of practice that are constructed by members as they establish roles and relationships, norms and expectations, rights and obligations that constitute membership in the local group" (p. 8, in press). In data collection and analysis, I based my attempt to understand "what was happening?" in these flexible notions of culture and practice.

The sociologist Becker (1998) argues that when ethnographers enter fields of study, they enter with certain images or pictures of how the world works. These images do not consist of a clearly articulated theory that ethnographers impose on research situations, but rather as a sort of guide that creates and clarifies the way ethnographers construct the logic of their research. In my case, the research process was not guided by a particular unified theory, but was influenced by the way teachers have been theorized and viewed in traditional policy literature.

My "images" influenced the lens I used to select, interpret, and analyze the events of the work lives of the teachers. Dyson (1993) argues that to truly understand the literacy development of students, researchers must situate themselves in the social worlds of the students they study. The same is true of teachers. To truly understand the realities of how a new educational policy shapes the work lives of teachers requires researchers to situate themselves in the lives of teachers—their classrooms, their meetings, their opinions, and their professional relationships with other members of the school community. While the need as a researcher to situate myself in the work lives of teachers was not a theory that I imposed on Walton Unified School District, it was the guiding image I kept in the forefront of my mind as I conducted the research.

Situating my focus on the work lives of teachers allowed me to examine policy implementation from the ground up. I attempted to see policy as more than an input-output process. Rather than searching for causal realities, I was able—through ethnography—to see components of social process and practice that influence the nature and context of policy. Erickson (1986) argues that interpretive research approaches focus on "issues of content rather than procedure" (p. 21). This distinction, he claims, allows the researcher to focus on key aspects of educational situations. Two of the aspects Erickson highlights are "the nature of the classroom as socially and culturally organized environments and the nature of the meaning-perspectives of teacher and learner as intrinsic to the educational process" (p. 121). Erickson (1986) then presents a list of questions that can best be answered by fieldwork. His questions raise central theoretical and methodological concerns for my research. The questions are grounded in what Emerson, Fretz, and Shaw (1995) call "the understanding and pursuing the meanings of individual participants." For this study, two of Erickson's (1986) questions were foundational:

> What is happening, specifically, in social action that takes place in this particular setting?
> How is what is happening in this setting as a whole (i.e., the classroom) related at other system levels outside the setting (e.g., the school building, a child's family, the school setting, federal government mandates regarding mainstreaming)? (p. 21)

These two questions guided my examination of the teachers' experience of the new policy context created by Proposition 227. In the spirit of understanding how "other system levels" were related to what was happening in the classroom, I situated myself in the lives of four teachers from two schools in Walton Unified School District. My focus was to make apparent *how* and *what* happened *in* and *out* of the classroom was related to the way teachers understood and experienced Proposition 227 implementation.

RESEARCH SITE, PARTICIPANTS AND METHOD

In order to understand the policy-to-practice connection as it relates to language policy, I traced the decisions and actions made by one school district. I trace the decision-making process at multiple levels—each a part of a progressively smaller unit of organization. They include: the district, two elementary schools in the district, and two teachers at each school and their classrooms.

Walton Unified School District

Walton Unified School District is situated in a small agricultural community in the California's Central Valley. Approximately 10,400 people live in the town, which is surrounded by fields of apricots, tomatoes, and other crops. A large frozen foods factory dominates the flat landscape of the town. The district contains around 3500 students. Approximately 62% of the students are Hispanic, and around 32% of the students are classified as LEP by the district.

In Garcia & Curry-Rodriquez (2001), the Curriculum Director and Superintendent of the "Walton Unified School District" were interviewed about district-wide implementation of the mandates of Proposition 227. In the weeks preceding the passage of Proposition 227, the two began discussions about how to implement Proposition 227. The curriculum director acknowledged in the interview that Open Valley and Westway, the two focal schools in the study, had very different opinions about Proposition 227. The Superintendent said he knew Westway administrators and some of the staff wanted to use Proposition 227 as a way to eliminate bilingual programs at their school, while the teachers of Open Valley wanted to pursue the parental waiver and maintain their bilingual program. The ideological differences about the benefits of primary language instruction were matched at the district level—the Superintendent is a long-time bilingual education supporter, and the Curriculum Director was identified by the Superintendent as an English-only advocate. Given their ideological rift, the two decided to give individual schools the choice of how they wanted to implement Proposition 227.

The Schools

Open Valley and Westway are very different schools. Westway Elementary is located on a tree-lined street a few blocks from the small business district of the town. It is a K-3 school with a sprawling campus the size of three city blocks. A total of 936 students attend the school with 68.6% of them receiving free or reduced lunch. The school has a Hispanic enrollment of 66.1% and a white enrollment of 33%. The school has an LEP population of 37.2%.

In the 1998-1999 academic year, Westway had only two teachers who were fluent speakers of Spanish. Although California Department of Education statistics indicate that 16 teachers were offering classes with primary language support, the majority of that instruction was carried out by bilingual aides. In the first year of Proposition 227 implementation, the school principal decided to eliminate the school's bilingual program. All language arts instruction at Westway is being done with the Open Court Reading series. During the 1999-2000 school year, four of the school's teachers were native speakers of Spanish.

Open Valley is a very different place. The campus is small in comparison to Westway's and houses grades K-6. The school is comprised by two parallel rows of classrooms with windows facing the agricultural fields surrounding the school. Adjacent to the school is a small migrant/agricultural farm-worker community. Of the school's 254 students, all qualify for free or reduced lunch and 93.3% are Hispanic. The school has an LEP population of 66.1%. Unlike Westway, Open Valley has at least one native Spanish-speaking teacher at each grade level. To avoid having to re-seek the waivers, the school applied for and received Charter status.

The Four Focal Teachers

In this section, I will describe relevant information about the four focal teachers of this study. The descriptions of the teachers are constructed using all sources of fieldnote data. I will first profile the two teachers from Westway and then describe the two teachers from Open Valley.

Westway: Celia. In her third year teaching at Westway, Celia, who was born in Mexico, is the most experienced native Spanish speaking teacher at the school. In her mid-20s, Celia holds a BCLAD certificate. She began teaching at Westway as a district intern and took full control of a classroom at the beginning of the next calendar year. She has always worked with grades 1 or 2. During the study (1999-2000 academic school year), Celia taught a 1st and 2nd grade split class.

Celia was a perpetually energetic and vivacious person. She frequently referred to her students as "my little guys" and approached her task with good humor and genuine enjoyment. She was constantly in very good spirits, and seemed to transmit an effervescent energetic quality to her students, who seemed to enjoy their time with her.

Celia was a eager and very forthcoming participant in this research. During my visits to her classroom, she would frequently tell me as an aside, "I got something I really have to tell. Wait until you hear this." Celia frequently volunteered vital information about the education of culturally and linguistically diverse students at the school.

Celia had strong collegial relations with many of the teachers on the primary side. In the lunch room and at teacher meetings, she was often at the center of professional and social conversations.

Westway: Connie. In her mid-30s, Connie had been teaching at the school for 11 years. In her first year at Westway, she had been assigned a bilingual class. After teaching in the program a few years, she was recruited to complete her LDS credential. For the past 11 years, Connie had always been assigned a bilingual classroom. The structure of the former bilingual program placed the responsibility of primary language literacy development on the school's bilingual teaching assistants. Consequently, during literacy instruction, Connie worked with the native-English speaking students in her classroom while the bilingual students worked with the teaching assistant. During the 1999-2000 academic year, Connie taught 3rd grade.

Connie, a Portuguese-American, took pride in her parents' accomplishments and achievements in America. Connie had some command of Spanish and exclusively spoke English in the classroom. She was highly critical of other teachers who used a great deal of Spanish in their classrooms.

During my observations, Connie frequently looked or indicated that she was frustrated. She noted that this year had been one of her worst years of teaching. She seemed to be balancing her frustrations and her earnest desire to help her students. The combination at times made Connie seem distant in the classroom.

Connie was not an especially gregarious person with her colleagues. While she had cordial relations with most of the members of the school community, she seemed a private person. She noted that she was not overly enthusiastic about collaborating with other teachers. Although she was quite cordial in meetings, she was usually quiet and rarely shared comments about her room or students.

Open Valley: Angelica.   A fifth-year teacher, Angelica came to teaching through her involvement in a migrant education program as an undergraduate. Although she was only in her late-20s, she had taught Sunday School for 12 years. She credited her experience with the migrant education program and her work in Sunday School as having a large influence on her teaching. She was born in Mexico, but attended school in California when her parents immigrated. During the year of the study, Angelica taught a 2nd grade bilingual class.

Angelica was a deeply committed and highly skilled teacher. Although she ended each day by hugging each student, her demeanor in the classroom was quite serious and professional. She frequently noted, "I speak very fast, so the kids know they just have to keep up with me." She did, and they did. She was frequently referred to by other members of the district and school as an excellent teacher.

During instruction, Angelica seldom wasted a minute of time. Her classroom was a very well ordered and efficient place where students were rarely off task. For her part, Angelica kept a highly energetic stance in her teaching.

Angelica had very close relations with many of the teachers and parents at the school. She helped to organize after school socials with the other teachers. Regarding parents, she said, "I need them more than they need me." This statement was indicative of Angelica's orientation in the classroom—she was connected to the cultural and social lives of her students.

Open Valley: Elisa.   Born in Mexico, Elisa was educated in California and grew up in the Central Valley. She had been a teacher for four years—all of them at Open Valley and each in a different grade. During the 1999-2000 academic year, Elisa taught a 3rd grade bilingual classroom.

Elisa's decision to enter teaching was closely related to her experiences as a child, which she considered very sheltered. Although she took a great deal of pride in her Mexican heritage, she felt that the culture of her family limited the potential growth of women. She remembered "always wanting to make a difference," but her parents were not comfortable with her "going off" and leaving the immediate sphere of the family. As an undergraduate, she traveled to Oaxaca to work in a community development project. She returned from the trip energized and became involved at Open Valley as a district intern. That position eventually led to full-time employment. While she was teaching, she returned to the university and completed her BCLAD credential.

Elisa seemed genuinely to enjoy her job. She was frequently surprised or amused by what her students did or said. She had a relaxed and comfortable interaction style with her class.

Although she was a dedicated teacher, Elisa envisioned herself leaving the classroom to pursue some other line of work that would allow her to help more people in a dramatic fashion. Often, our conversations about what type of career she would like to have revealed her desire to take on active roles in politics and social issues concerning the Latino community.

Gaining Access

Gaining permission to study the local enactment of policy in Walton Unified School District was made easier due to data collected in the district during the Garcia, et al., study, which took place during the 1998-1999 academic year. During the Spring of 1999, I traveled to Walton and interviewed Celia, Elizabeth, and Angelica. The district had been selected for the Garcia, et al., research based upon the authors' knowledge that there were unique features in the district's implementation procedures for Proposition 227. For the Garcia, et al., study, I spent two weeks in the district. In addition to interviews, I observed each of the interviewed teachers' classrooms.

Based upon the relationships that I had made during my visit, I contacted Celia, Elizabeth, and Angelica at each school in the closing days of the1998-1999 academic year and asked if they would be willing to allow me to examine how issues of Proposition 227 unfold over a prolonged period of time in their classroom. The teachers agreed to participate in the study. In addition, I contacted the Superintendent of district and asked if he would permit me to spend a year in the two schools.

At the opening of the 1999-2000 school year, I arranged appointments with the two principals at the schools, the curriculum director, the superintendent, and 3 of the 4 teachers whom I had interviewed in the Spring of 1998. With each individual, I detailed the nature of my work, my research questions, and what their participation in the study would mean. With all potential participants, I stressed the fact that I was not interested in evaluating a particular teaching methodology or a particular course of action in response Proposition 227, but, rather, was interested in understanding how the new law was influencing teachers' work and classroom practice. Each individual agreed to participate in the study. There was little hesitation on the part of the teachers. From my interviews of the teachers in the Spring of 1999, it was clear that the teachers had a great deal that they wanted to say about how the changes brought about by Proposition 227 had influenced their professional lives.

At Open Valley, one of the teachers I had interviewed in the Spring of 1999 had left the school. Because Westway contains only grades K-3, I recruited Open Valley's third grade bilingual teacher to participate in the study. My selection of the teachers was largely influenced by my participation in the Garcia, et al., study. I used the same selection process for the fourth teacher in the study as Garcia, et al.:

> The teacher is currently classified as a bilingual teacher, or the teacher was classified as a bilingual teacher prior to Proposition 227 implementation.

> The teacher works in a classroom where at least 50% of the students are classified as Limited English Proficient.

A Note on Terms

In my attempt to build a local understanding of the influence of Proposition 227, I use the local vocabulary to refer to the students who made up the four classrooms of study. These terms differed at each school. The culturally and linguistically diverse students at Westway were most often referred to as "English Language Learners"—ELLs. The acronym "ELLs" was often truncated to "ELs." At Open Valley, culturally and linguistically diverse were most often referred to as "the bilingual students" or "Latino students." In the theoretical discussions which do not directly relate to findings or the legal language of Proposition 227, I will use the expression "culturally and linguistically diverse students" as in Garcia (1999). The expression moves away from classifying students in terms of English ability (e.g., non-native speaker and limited English proficient), and moves toward seeing the language and culture of diverse students as an important instructional resource.

Data Collection

The period of study was the 1999-2000 school year. I began data collection in September of 1999 and concluded in late May 2000. Because data collection was based on "developing the story as it is experienced by participants" (Woods, 1994), I used multiple sources of data to build this picture. These included classroom observations, interviews, observations of teachers' meetings, and collections of cultural artifacts. I divided my research into two phases: data collected during first semester of the 1999-2000 academic year was labeled Phase 1 (PH # 1), data collected during the second semester was called Phase 2 (PH # 2). Throughout the book, I indicate the phase from which the data were collected for the purpose of exposing how teachers negotiated curricular decisions over the course of the school year.

During Phase 1 of the data collection, I observed each teacher's classroom a minimum of 10 times. I used the first three observations to familiarize myself with the classroom routines of the teachers. After these initial classroom observations, I conducted informal unstructured interviews with each of the teachers. I designed these brief interviews to assist me in selecting the focal classroom literacy events. Using the knowledge I had gained from these initial observations and the teachers' perspectives about what constituted the most important aspects of the curriculum for the first or second language development of their students, I selected a set of focal classroom literacy events to observe for each teacher. These focal literacy events were the principal source of all classroom observation data. Focal event selection differed from teacher to teacher because each teacher had different ideas about which events were seminal in their students' development. During Phase 2, I observed each teacher a minimum of 8 times.

During classroom observations, I took detailed "scratch notes" (Emerson, et al., 1995) chronicling the "action" of classroom events. My observations in each classroom generally lasted between one and two hours. During Phase 1, I used a handheld recorder with a built-in microphone to record the oral communication in the class. During Phase 2, hoping to increase the sound quality of the taped observations, I arranged for the teachers to wear wireless microphones during observations.

I used my scratch notes and audio recording to write detailed accounts of the literacy events I observed. Constructing fieldnotes was a time-consuming process, typically taking between three and five hours for each observation. During the writing of the fieldnotes, I attempted not to use evaluative language or to impose my interpretations on events. As Emerson, et al., (1995) argue, to capture what is out there, the ethnographer tries to:

> Construct detailed accounts of observations and experiences of what is "out there." At this point, too much reflection distracts or even paralyzes; one tries to write without editing, to produce detailed description without worrying about analytic import or connections, to describe what happened without too much self-conscious reflection. (p. 64)

Moving away from evaluative language in description of literacy events forced me to provide vivid descriptions of classroom practice. Rather than use labels such as "good practice" or "bad practice," I attempted to describe as fully as possible the action inside the classrooms.

The classrooms I observed were dynamic places. Attempting to portray that dynamism in writing was a difficult task. To give a feel of the nature of teacher and student interaction in this report, I will present teacher and student interaction in three-columned transcripts. The first column contains the words of the teacher in a particular event, the second the words of the student. Each line in the column represents a moment of time. If the teacher and a student spoke at the same time, their dialog occupies the same vertical line of the transcript. Their physical actions or any other contextual building descriptions appear in the third column. Like the dialogue, they are time sensitive. That is, if a teacher said "x" and did "y" at the same time they appear on the same vertical line in the three-columned transcript.

In addition to classroom observations, semi-structured ethnographic interviews were a major source of data for this project. Each of the four focal teachers were interviewed twice—once in Phase 1 and once in Phase 2 of the research. The interviews lasted between one and two hours for each teacher. In addition to the teachers, I interviewed the superintendent, the district's curriculum director, and the two principals at the school. Each interview was audio recorded and transcribed.

A third set of data came from grade level, school-wide, and district-wide meetings that the teachers attended. I attended meetings that related to literacy instruction and the education of the culturally and linguistically diverse students in the district. These included planning meetings, grade level curriculum meetings, school-wide governance meetings, and district-wide English Language Advisory Council meetings. During the meetings, I took "scratch notes" and used them to compile field notes similar to my classroom observations. My point of interest was not the meeting as a whole, but the focal teachers' relations and behavior in these meetings. In total, I observed six meetings at Westway, seven at Open Valley, and two district-wide meetings.

A final source of data were cultural artifacts from the classroom, school, and district levels pertaining to Proposition 227 and the literacy instruction of the culturally diverse students. I collected meeting agendas, Proposition 227 implementation plan documents, school governance documents, curriculum guidelines, and literacy material.

My Role as Participant Observer. During data collection, I was a fairly strict observer of classroom events and did not have extended interaction with students or the teacher. If students asked me a question, I answered. In all cases, I answered students questions in the language it was asked. During Phase 1 of the research, I spent afternoons in the four focal teachers' classrooms as a volunteer. During these 45-minute "volunteer sessions," I worked with small groups or one-on-one with students. Although my volunteer sessions were not a formal part of data collection, they often informed my writing of field notes by giving me a deeper understanding of the children. Additionally, my volunteer work gave me first-hand experiences with the curricular materials the teachers were using.

I spent a great deal of time with Angelica, Elisa, Connie, and Celia. Although I attempted to structure my participation in the schools as an observer, the teachers often used me as a sounding board for their concerns and wishes at their respective schools. They asked me questions, and sought my advice on some issues. As I will discuss in Chapters three, four, and five, their work worlds were not without tension and conflict—professional, social, ideological, and racial. In my discussions with the teachers after classroom observations, during lunch, or after meetings, they discussed these tensions with me. At Open Valley, the two teachers—Angelica and Elisa—commented on their deep commitment to bilingual education and their dissatisfaction with the positions held by many individuals in their district—including many of the teachers at Westway—regarding bilingual education. At Westway, teachers often spoke to me of a school district that "had done too much for the bilingual bunch." At Open Valley, I spoke Spanish. At Westway, I spoke English. As I observed the ideological conflicts and tensions Proposition 227 helped create, I realized that, in many ways, I was whomever the teachers wanted me to be. At Open Valley, I was a Spanish-speaker and former teacher who had worked with immigrant populations. At Westway, I was a white male who did not look like their Latino students or the Latino teachers at Open Valley.

Data Analysis

In writing fieldnotes from classroom literacy events, teacher meetings, and interviews, I attempted to create a detailed description of "what is out there." Such a description allowed me to switch from a "writing mode" in the construction of field notes to a "reading mode" during the analysis of fieldnotes (Emerson, et al., 1995). During data collection, I wrote brief in-process memos containing questions I had about particular events in the data. In these memos, I pursued hunches I had about occurrences in the classroom and the work lives of the four teachers in the study. These in-process memos were the basis of generating interview questions. In addition, the in-process memos served as the construct with which I interrogated, refined, and re-saw the larger research question guiding this project.

After I left the field in late May, I completed a close reading of the entire set of field notes looking for "certain words, phrases, patterns of behavior, subjects' way of thinking, and events that stand out" (Bogdan and Biklen, 1992, p. 166). During the initial read-through, I asked questions of the data that centered on building an understanding of what it meant to be a teacher and experience the new policy context created by Proposition 227. To each question, I wrote brief analytic commentary grounded in the data. Some questions were general:

> Why did I include this in my fieldnotes?
> How does this quote or fieldnote observation relate to Proposition 227?
> Why does this fieldnote excerpt surprise me or not surprise me?

Others were closely tied to the research questions guiding the project:

> Why do the teachers use "war" and "boxing" metaphors to describe their curricular struggles?
> How is Open Valley's Charter status a response to Proposition 227?
> How do the teachers talk about literacy and English instruction? Does their talk reflect the way it looks in classroom practice?
> How do the teachers view their places in the district?

I did not limit the types or nature of questions I asked of the data, nor was I overly concerned that my answers to the questions directly aligned with my research questions. The process of asking questions of the data and writing analytic memos served as the basis for my open coding of the data, which in turn served as the basis of focused coding.

Drawing upon fieldnote excerpts I had written about in my memos, I selected four literacy events per teacher to open code. Open coding entailed a line-by-line reading and coding of my notes. I wrote phrases in the margins of the notes which were based upon some of the analytic work I had done in the "read through and questions phase" of analysis. My purpose of open coding was two-fold: first, to develop the language and themes that would guide my focused coding; and second, to begin to see like events and patterns emerge and change over time.

Using the open codes, I created focused codes that were aligned with my research questions. I used the focus codes to code the entire classroom observation data set. The focused codes included five categories:

1. Instructional role of Spanish and/or English
2. Student participation in teacher-run literacy events
3. Nature of teacher questions in literacy events
4. Framing of teacher-run events
5. Reading event interaction

The coding categories were based upon my research questions and the open coding. In order to build a more emic perspective, I used teachers' words as the specific codes under each category. After developing a coding system for classroom events, I conducted a detailed, line-by-line focused coding of all observation data. This coding set the stage for my development and organization of the data in the findings chapters in this book. The coding process served as a physical and analytic sorting of the data.

My coding of the teacher meetings and interviews followed a similar process: a close reading, followed by open coding, followed by focused coding. Coding of these data sources emphasized building an understanding of teachers' purposes during literacy instruction. Additionally, I was concerned with building an understanding of how teachers perceived Proposition 227 and experienced its implementation in their district and schools. Focused coding categories included:

1. The structure and implementation of Proposition 227
2. The individual characteristics of teachers
3. Impeding or facilitating teacher agency
4. Teacher's purpose in instruction
5. The way teachers were organized and experienced the decision making structure of the school

I used the interview and teacher meeting data to help interpret classroom observation data as my level of analysis centered on the teacher's views of Proposition 227, their construction of literacy instruction to meet the needs of their students, their perceptions of their instructional practice, and the relationships between these.

In the following three chapters, I describe the major findings of this research. I describe how the teachers experienced the new policy context created by Proposition 227, and examine how instances of classroom practice illuminate the role teachers play in the reform process.

CHAPTER 4

The Proposition 227
Policy Context:
Teacher Perceptions and Behavior

I don't think there has been a real change in relations between the teachers and the district administration because of Proposition 227 because the schools were very different to begin with. Even before 227, Open Valley was very pro-bilingual education, had bilingual teachers, and the community was very involved in their program. At Westway, the community wasn't as supportive, it wasn't a comprehensive program, so they were already set up towards more of an English Language Development model. It's just that Prop. 227 made it very easy for us to say: Now it's your choice. (Curriculum Director, December 10, 1999, Interview)

In discussing the influence Proposition 227 implementation had on relations among Westway, Open Valley, and the district office, Walton's Curriculum Director "Nancy Ketchem" stressed that district-level decisions created minimal tension in the district because they were based on existing instructional strengths and ideologies at the two schools. From the district perspective, Proposition 227 implementation did not cause a major disturbance because the district developed a plan that fit existing climates at the school sites.

41

Nancy Katchem's comments were echoed by the Walton Superintendent, who noted that the differences between the two school communities—Westway and Open Valley—were the guiding reason why the district's response to Proposition 227 allowed flexibility at the local school level:

> Westway tended to use a more English orientation in their bilingual program prior to 227. It was very transitional in nature. What I found after 227 passed was that the principal and teachers at the site felt that the best instructional design for them and the school would be to move into more English Only. There's some factors related to the community, there's some factors related to the number of certificated staff that are on board and there's probably some factors related to the principal's own preference of instruction. (Superintendent, Interview, PH # 2)

Discussing Open Valley, the Superintendent explained that a long commitment to "bilingual issues and multiculturalism" and a group of "activist teachers and parents" created a very positive environment for continuing bilingual education. Although the two school communities seemed similar demographically, the Superintendent contended that they were quite different in fact. The differences came into play the summer after Proposition 227 had passed as the Curriculum Director was creating the district's implementation plan. She noted that the district "wanted to give the schools as much flexibility as possible within the law." The district administration's emphasis on choice and flexibility indicated that—at least in Walton—what has and was occurring at the local school level entered into the decision-making process at the district level. While giving schools latitude was the district's decision, it was influenced by the climate of local schools—a climate in large part created by the site administrators and teachers.

Even though many of the Proposition 227 implementation discussions in Walton were couched in terms of choice and flexibility, further examination of the teachers' experiences of the district and school structures indicates that choice and flexibility were not experienced equally by the four teachers in this study. Although district decisions about Proposition 227 did fit the local climate and instructional realities at the schools, the local schools were not monolithic entities. District-level and school-level decisions regarding Proposition 227 organized teachers in particular ways. Part of this organization was related to the structural arrangements that facilitated the execution of those decisions. These structural arrangements, when viewed in combination with the individual qualities of the four teachers, served to create the nature of instructional practice in the schools. In this chapter, I will consider how decisions made at the district level about Proposition 227 allowed or impeded teacher-agency, and how the organization of the teachers within the district and school sites mediated the nature of the implementation of Proposition 227.

DISTRICT LEVEL DECISIONS: ENABLERS AND DISABLERS

In order to understand how district decisions regarding Proposition 227 influenced the nature of teaching in Walton Unified School District, I will further explore the district's implementation plan. The emphasis on flexibility and choice expressed by the Superintendent and the Curriculum Director was evident in the document the district produced to guide local schools in their implementation of the law. The district implementation plan allowed schools to choose among four program types:

> English Development Program—This is the program developed as a result of Proposition 227. All ELs (English Learners) identified as Level 1, 2, or low 3 will be placed in this class.
> SDAIE Program—This is mainstream class designed for ELs identified as intermediate fluency.
> Mainstream Program—This is the regular District Program.
> Spanish Bilingual Program—Instruction and materials are in English and Spanish.

(Walton Unified Implementation Plan, 1998)

Although the language of choice and flexibility surrounded nearly all district level discussions of Proposition 227, both the Superintendent and the Curriculum Director knew which way Westway and Open Valley would go. At both schools, teachers and administrators had left little doubt that they were headed in opposite directions regarding the education of their Latino students.

It was in this context that the four teachers in the study made decisions about their literacy instruction. When the district's implementation plan for Proposition 227 met with the organizational structures and cultures of the two schools in the study, issues related to the education of the Latino students emerged and faded in new ways. These issues unfolded differently for each of the four teachers. This difference was related to both who the teachers were—their individual educational experiences, their professional experiences, and their political ideologies—and the context in which they taught. Several factors determined these contexts: the role of the principal in making decisions about literacy instruction, the language arts series used by each school, the role of outside consultants, and grant monies.

As teachers' roles evolved in course of Proposition 227 implementation, certain types of action, or agency, became possible. Other types of action became more difficult. At the simplest level, the new policy context created moments when teachers felt they could take steps to address or resolve educational issues that existed either inside or outside their classrooms. The teachers' feelings regarding these issues were ultimately related to the nature of their school's post-Proposition 227 direction. For these reasons, I call these features of the policy context, *policy enablers*. A second feature of the new policy context created a feeling amongst teachers that they had little room or ability to address a particular issues. I call these features of context, *policy disablers*. The terms policy enabler and policy disabler are not meant to indicate the success or failure of a particular teacher action; rather, they highlight the nature of the situation and policy context in which teachers found themselves.

At each school site, different kinds of policy enablers and policy disablers were the realities of the teachers' work days. The policy enablers and disablers influenced the way the teachers saw their lives in the classroom and how they behaved in school meetings. I will first examine these issues as they unfolded at Westway Elementary and then consider the issues at Open Valley.

Westway: English Only and Open Court

Teacher positioning at Westway was related to four factors: the district's policy of choice and flexibility, Westway's decision to fully implement the English Development Model, the school's adoption of a new language arts program, and the manner in which the language arts program was implemented. Each of these four factors created and limited certain types of space for teacher action. Before examining the experiences of the two focal teachers in the new policy context created by Proposition 227, I will describe the school's move to English Only and its adoption of Open Court as the school-wide literacy series.

The Move to English Only. The decision to adopt an English Only model was made unilaterally by the school's veteran principal, "Beverly Elmherst." Both Celia and Connie recalled receiving a letter a few months before the opening of school in the fall of 1998 informing them of the school's new program. Mrs. Elmherst was a strong and charismatic leader who frequently made top-down decisions at the school. Although the school's new direction was ultimately subject to district approval, the nature of the school's old program left the district little option other than to approve the English Only plan. The Superintendent explained it this way:

> The old program was neither well designed, appropriately staffed or implemented consistently. So when they came up with the English Only design, although I had some initial reservations, I did feel that they were going to be more consistent in instruction and have a staff to implement English Only. (Superintendent, Interview, PH # 2)

The Superintendent also explained that Westway had not met the district's criteria of an adequate program when it was using a bilingual model. The new policy context created by the district's implementation of Proposition 227 was a policy enabler for Westway's principal. The school's inadequate program prior to 1999 and the district's emphasis on flexibility allowed Mrs. Elmherst to move the school in the direction of English Only.

While Mrs.Elmherst was optimistic about the new direction, she acknowledged that her decision affected teachers in a variety of ways.

> I think for the teachers who were B-CLAD trained or who are
> themselves native speakers, who had gone through schooling
> where they had no Spanish instruction, it was difficult. I think
> they felt like they were put in the corner. They were the most
> apprehensive about how this was going to work. (Beverly,
> Interview, PH #2)

Despite her concerns about how native-speaking teachers might feel,
the failure of the past program as well as her preference for English
instruction made for an easy choice to move in a new direction. With a
smile on her face and a hint of joy in her voice Mrs. Elmherst said,
"The California populace has made their decision, they've voted, so we
have to do the best we can for the kids."

Open Court: The Rest of the Story Programmatic directions for the
school's native-speaking student population were only part of the story
at Westway. The school's adoption of Open Court Collections for
Young (hereafter, Open Court) as the language arts series as well as
their participation in a $300,000 grant provided by The Packard
Foundation completed the Proposition 227 story at Westway. Open
Court uses explicit teacher-directed instruction to teach phonemic
awareness, phonics, and reading comprehension. During the
instructional components of the program, which include teacher-
directed writing and reading exercises, and skills practice drills,
teachers use scripts for all teacher questions, prompts, and responses.
During blending, a center piece of the program, teachers read all sounds
of a word and have students repeat them. Reading and writing activities
are tightly controlled by the teacher.

   In addition to providing the Open Court materials, the grant paid
for two literacy coach positions filled by senior teachers at the
school—neither of whom had extensive experiences with ELLs. The
grant also resulted in regular visits from two "Open Court Experts" as
they were called by the teachers and principal. The Open Court
Experts' involvement in literacy instruction at the school ranged from
the development of the school-wide pacing schedule that all teachers in
the school had to follow to observations of individual teachers, which
frequently lead to recommended changes in instruction that teachers
were compelled to make.

The decisions made by the Open Court Experts were enforced by the school's two literacy coaches. These decisions included: the physical arrangement of teachers' rooms, the elimination of small group instruction, and the monitoring teacher language use in instruction. Although many of the decisions made by the Open Court Experts were not explicitly mandated by the Open Court Program, there was little distinction between the "Experts" and the "Program" for the teachers at Westway. The control arrangements were a source of frustration for teachers at the school. Frequently, many of the teachers—both mainstream as well as English Development teachers—made sarcastic and hostile comments regarding the role of the Open Court "Experts" at the school.

The school's implementation of Proposition 227 and the decision-making structures had a major influence on the way the two teachers in the study experienced the new policy context. A primary feature of this context was related to the district's belief that the teachers were part of an inadequate bilingual program. The perception of their past inadequacy contributed to the view that the teachers at the school needed less autonomy and more oversight. To this end, the principal described her main role as controlling her teachers and ensuring they were implementing Open Court properly. Beverly described her role as a mother keeping her children in line or as a teacher making sure that "100% of the kids get what I am teaching." While these metaphors were characterized by a compassionate stance towards her charges, not all of Beverly's comments about her role were mild. When describing how she kept her large school staff committed to the ideals of the program, she explained:

> So how do I do it? I just keep hammering away at them saying: You've gotta do it. You're cheating your kids if you don't and if you don't recognize the teachers at the school who are having success with the program. We have the teachers paired into little planning teams that meet once a week. We post their scores for each end of the unit reading assessment. There's assessments so we are posting those on the wall. (Beverly, Interview, PH # 2)

The need to control the teachers at Westway was supported—at least implicitly—by the district view that what the program had previously lacked was consistency. In response, Beverley viewed her main role as ensuring that teachers merely executed the program as they were told by the Open Court Experts. Beverly believed that such a course of action by the teachers would address both the English language literacy needs of the students as well as the school's sagging test scores. As Beverly explained, "I keep telling them. Teach the program; it's all there." Her confidence was buoyed by her perception of the program's ability to meet the needs of ELL students:

> I think one thing that's kind of helped the staff is the fact that the people who have come to help us this year have made it real clear that it doesn't matter if a child can speak English or not. That if he uses the program and you do it correctly, then we are going to see success. (Beverly, Interview, PH # 2)

Beverly felt that because teachers had bought into the program and had in fact seen this success, a sense of optimism pervaded the teachers' views about their students' progress. Much of the talk of measuring that success rested exclusively with the SAT 9. The belief by the Open Court Experts—which had in large part been adopted by Beverly and the school's literacy coaches—that the language needs of the ELL students were met by a "correct" implementation of the program worked to position both Connie and Celia as Open Court teachers and not as English language development teachers.

While their classrooms were designated English Development rooms, the nature of their positioning at the school was no different than any of the other teachers—their main role was to execute the Open Court program. The way the two women experienced this positioning and the types of action they took as a result is related to their individual qualities as teachers. Because this examination of teacher positioning centers on the individual qualities of teachers, I will examine each teacher separately.

Celia: Tension, Contradictions and the Search for "Safe Space"

The connection between Celia's positioning at the school site and the influence of Proposition 227 on literacy instruction at Westway was underscored by a seemingly contradictory arrangement between her primary role as Open Court teacher and her role as a leader in Latino student concerns at the school. Like all teachers at Westway, Celia was primarily responsible for implementing the Open Court program according to the plans developed by the Open Court Experts. At times, this reality was a policy disabler for Celia. She noted being so "burned-out" by the Open Court decision-making structures that she felt nearly paralyzed at times. These feelings were rooted in her fear of doing something that would be interpreted or identified as "wrong" by the Open Court Experts. This fear translated to her views about language use. She explained, "For myself, it was hard to keep the students' attention. I myself wasn't sure how much Spanish I could use or how much translation I could use to be able to express the lessons to them." While Celia experienced a sort of paralysis stemming from Proposition 227 and the school's language arts series, she was also being asked by her principal and other Latina teachers to serve as a spokesperson for issues related to the school's Latino community.

Policy Disabler Meets a Proud Bilingual. The contradictions of her roles played out as Celia navigated her way through the many pressing issues her students faced. Her feelings of paralysis and lack of autonomy influenced the way she was able to deal with issues affecting her students. Towards the end of the academic year, the parent of one of Celia's most impressive success stories, Lucia, raised concerns that Lucia no longer wanted to read in Spanish to her at home. In addition, Lucia refused to speak to her mother in Spanish. While Celia concluded that Lucia's behavior was entirely related to the instructional realties of her classroom and the over all climate of the school, she felt there was little she could do and that "her hands were tied." During the year, she devoted time to Spanish read out-loud, but this was limited to an occasional 10-minute slot per week. Her position as a teacher of Open Court left her little instructional room to address this issue. In this case, the features of context created by the use of Open Court at the school limited the action Celia could take. Although she held a personal belief in the value of maintaining a first language, the new policy context left with her with few direct ways to address this problem.

While she felt powerless in the classroom, Celia did write a letter to all her parents encouraging them to read to their children in Spanish. Her frustration with this situation—a school climate that played a part in a student's refusal to speak Spanish and her limited instructional outlets to address the problem—left her feeling powerless within the existing arrangement at Westway:

> If I had to do this again, I wouldn't want to do this with the program and with the restrictions that they have placed upon me as a teacher. They've chopped down all the sorts of the creativity and ideas that I have. They have just cut so many links to **m e**. They've made me feel very ineffective and powerless. I guess they've taken power away from me as teacher and that doesn't feel right. (Celia, Interview, PH #2)

In the case of her students' perceptions about their native language, Celia's individual quality of being a proud bilingual met with limited success in addressing the issues to her satisfaction. She understood the problem, having experienced language loss in her own family, but her positioning within the school left her with unsatisfactory means to resolve the issue for her students. Celia's reactions to the issue of language loss were indicative of her feelings regarding the more ideologically charged issues at the school. She deeply regretted the lack of a favorable climate for the school's Latina teachers and the school's less than receptive stance to the parents of her students. She felt some of the other non-native speaker teachers at the school held racist beliefs regarding the language and culture of the Latino students. Unfortunately, she felt there was little she could do to completely resolve these issues. For Celia, the features of Open Court and English Only limited the types of actions she felt she could take to address the needs of her students.

A Leader in the Classroom and School. While dealing with ideological issues often resulted in frustration for Celia, it was not the case that all of Celia's work at the school ended with unsatisfactory results and feelings of frustration. The times when Celia felt a sense of agency at the school were related to her positioning as an "expert" and a "leader" in the school. In her third full year as a teacher, Celia was the most experienced native-speaker of Spanish on the staff. In addition to this position of relative experience, she was considered by both the principal and the literacy coaches at the school to be one of the real strengths of the program for ELLs. By her colleagues—particularly her Latina colleagues—she was considered an instructional resource and was positioned as the senior spokesperson. Frequently, the other early primary teachers in the school would raise concerns first with Celia and ask that she take those concerns to the principal, which she frequently did.

Celia had become the voice for Latino issues in the school. The policy context created by the school's implementation of English Only and use of Open Court had left little official space to discuss issues not directly related to "doing the program." The void created by the shift away from traditional second language issues such as English language development, academic English, or instructional modifications for second language learners was a policy enabling feature of the new context. In the absence of any official discussion about these issues, Celia filled the gap. She discussed these issues with her colleagues and brought them to the attention of her principal.

For Celia, being positioned as an expert by her colleagues was not always comfortable. She frequently commented that she was only a third-year teacher and had a great deal to learn. In the first year under Proposition 227, Celia served as the translator at the meeting where the waiver process was explained to the parents. Celia recalled that Beverly was very heavy handed in her explanation about the new English Only program. Beverly's explanation left the parents little room to seek the waiver. At the meeting, Celia felt conflicted and wanted to share some of her own feelings about the role that an alternate to English Only could serve. Given her lack of tenure and her perception of her own inexperience, she translated Beverly's plan without adding her own thoughts. After the meeting, Celia reported that the district Superintendent told her that she should have let parents know a bit more about the waivers process. From that moment, Celia's work life was imbued with the tension of being viewed as an expert by certain school personnel and her own self doubt about that role.

For Celia, these doubts were rooted in her beliefs about the benefit of bilingual education as well as her own educational experience. As a student, Celia had been placed in English Only classrooms, and she described the experience as very isolating. She recalled not learning how to read until the fifth grade. Despite these hardships, she had succeeded, but she often wondered if the success was worth the pain.

These doubts were rooted in her belief about the benefits of primary language instruction, which had slowly grown stronger since the passage of Proposition 227. Initially, her feelings regarding the benefits of primary language instruction had ranged from "not necessary" to "could help," but by the end of the year her experience with a handful of new students who came to her room already reading in Spanish worked to deepen her belief that it was beneficial. She said:

> It's like it just reinforces that if they have their native language and can read, they transfer over those strategies to English so much faster than if you try and teach them from scratch (Celia, Interview, PH #2).

She described this realization as a "new learning." She applied her developing ideas in the way she conducted her classroom and the types of agency and action she took for her EL students.

Nature of Agency. Taking agency was a very measured type of action for Celia —a judicious and well thought out type of agency in which Celia waited for the right time and place to take action. She picked her battles. One example of her savvy was the way in which she described her implementation of Open Court—"pumping it up." Her attempt to "pump it up" was a strategy Celia hoped would buy her time in affecting real change regarding the education of EL students at the school:

> I wanted to be honest and be able to say to my principal: "Do you know what? I did it the way that you told me to and it didn't work." So I really wanted to try it their way [Open Court Experts], so I could say, "I tried it your way and it didn't work, this didn't work, and that didn't work. And, I believe I can do better. (Celia, Personal Conversation, PH #2).

Indeed, Celia took the advice from her Open Court Experts as well as her own literacy coaches very seriously. On several occasions after meetings with her literacy coach and the Open Court Experts, Celia commented to me that she had made a particular curricular change based upon feedback she had received.

While a close adherence to the way Open Court Experts and school administrators said the program should be conducted (this including the smallest of advice like the positioning of the sound spelling cards in the room to larger more significant curricular practices like the elimination of small group instruction) very much characterized Celia's classroom conduct, her desire to "not argue with the numbers" (Interview, PH #1) was rooted in Celia's attempt to change the nature of instruction at the school site. Her classroom did reflect the influence of the Open Court Experts and she felt that this would result in tangible failure that would give her some credibility when trying to change the nature of the program.

Celia hoped her faithful implementation of Open Court would afford her creditability with her principal when it came time to make decisions regarding next year's program. For Celia, the confluence of SAT 9 testing and the planned new arrangement for the grouping of ELL students created a space to exercise agency. The grant had paid for the scoring of the first grade SAT 9 scores. Only 7% of Celia's class were on grade level. These results were confirmation to Celia that the program and its implementation were a failure. She explained, "Having in mind that my door was open and anytime these people wanted to come in and see Open Court they could, I was faithful to the program. I wanted to say I tried it, and it didn't work." The results of the test scores were the proof Celia needed that the program had not worked.

At nearly the same time that the school received the first-grade test results, the school was finalizing a plan that would disperse all the ELL children—with the exception of Kindergarten students—to mainstream classes. This meant that each teacher in the school would have six or seven ELL students. Celia believed that the limited success she had with the program was in large part related to the adaptations she made during instructional time and her ability to speak Spanish when the students were not understanding. Celia was concerned that the ELL students would not get the necessary support with the mainstream teachers—none of whom were native speakers of Spanish.

Celia's belief that the grouping arrangement was problematic was situated in her notion of what it meant to be a Latina teacher at the school. Celia frequently commented that there were many reasons the school had a very hard time retaining Latina teachers. Celia felt part of this had to do with the attitudes of her Anglo colleagues:

We [Latina teachers] always feel different here, because somehow we are made conscious of it. Sometimes there are just little comments in the lunch room when one of us brings in some food like, "Oh, what kind of food is that?" (Celia, Interview, PH #2)

She acknowledged that comments about food might seem trivial, but felt such comments belied deeper prejudice towards the culture and language of the Latina teachers at the school. Celia was concerned that the teachers making the comments would not be able to meet the needs of the school's native Spanish speaking students in the same way she had. She was concerned that Open Court Experts would call on teachers to just "teach the program" and the ELL students would get lost in the shuffle.

In an attempt to exercise agency at the school, Celia first took this concern to her literacy coach. She began the conversation with the coach by saying that only 7% of her students were at grade level and that made her very concerned about next year's planned mixing of the students. She was told "not to worry about it because next year she will have a mixed group." Celia had also made some comments to her principal—for whom she felt deep respect and admiration—but had not really "put it on the line for her." She also concluded that from what she could tell, "Beverly was just following [the directions] of the Open Court Experts."

Having attempted to exercise some agency at the local school level, but meeting with limited success given the structural realities of decision making and school priorities, Celia took her concerns to the end of the year English Language Advisory Committee (ELAC). The committee consisted of teachers from each of the district's schools who met to discuss issues related to the ELL students in the district. The meeting, which occurred shortly after the incident involving her literacy coach, seemed to be a sort of last ditch effort to stop the changes planned for next year.

The meeting was run by a district administrator—a confident and well-spoken women. After the group discussed its scheduled business, the leader of the meeting asked if there were any other concerns. Celia took a deep breath and swallowed hard. She embarked on what would be a 20-minute speech regarding her frustration during the year, her interaction with the decision-making structures at her school, and the vision of what she wanted her school to look like. She began:

> I don't know if this is exactly a part of this committee, but I don't know where else I could go with this, so I am going to raise it here with this committee. I have some real concerns about the EL kids being mainstreamed next year. We are hearing all of this stuff about how great the program is, and how great the SAT 9 scores are. My SAT 9 scores are not that way. Only 7% of my little guys are above grade level. And the way they are going to do this next year, I am just afraid we are going to have our little guys fall thought the cracks. I am worried that mainstream teachers are not going to address the needs of **my** students. (Celia, ELAC meeting, PH # 2)

Through her tears and with comments of support from the other members at the meeting, Celia chronicled how she had "been pushed and pushed" to follow the exact commands of the Open Court Experts. Her tears turned to anger and defiance as she claimed, "I know what they want, but I don't think I can do it for them."

In many ways the agency Celia attempted reveals the nature of who she is as a teacher, a person, and the structure of her work world. As a Latina teacher, Celia took great pride in being a role model for her students. She extended that pride to herself and to her peer-appointed role as the "vocal one in the EL group." Although these qualities influenced the types of issues she believed mattered at the school, in the end, her attempt at agency resulted in a great deal of frustration. Although she was constantly looking for that "safe place" to raise her concerns, she worked in a context in which there were precious few safe places. While her individual qualities might have supported advocacy for her Latino students, she was not able to completely supercede the structure in which she worked. Although she could not completely overcome the structure, she was, through her actions, able to bring issues to the school and district discourse that might otherwise have been excluded.

Summary of Celia's Role in Proposition 227 *Implementation.* Celia's experience of and actions within the decision-making structures at her school go a long way to complicate traditional conceptions of teachers' roles in the implementation of policy. Far from being a mere conductor of state, district, and school policy mandates, Celia worked to change the context and direction of the school's education of linguistically and culturally diverse students. For Celia, this was a two-year process over which her feelings and beliefs about bilingual education and her own role as a teacher evolved a great deal. Her experience of English Only and Open Court served to spark a new interest and a deepening commitment to the potential benefits of primary language instruction. While learning in the face of new policy has been explored in the literature (Jennings, 1996), Celia's experiences of the new policy context extended beyond learning into moments of action. Although she was not always able to accomplish her goals, her actions indicated that there were features of the new policy context that were policy enablers. Celia did not change the direction of the school's programmatic choices, but her actions shaped how the new policy context was experienced.

Connie: Doing English Only; Doing Open Court

While Celia was continually searching for safe places to raise issues related to the EL students at the school, Connie maintained a very low profile when it came to such issues. This low profile was related to both who she was as a person and her experiences with the decision-making structure at the school. Connie's work as a teacher was entirely consumed by Open Court and the pacing schedule. This focus on Open Court shifted emphasis away from issues related to the linguistic and social realties of the second language development of the Latino students in the school. For Connie, two features of the new policy context, the move to English Only and the implementation of Open Court, were responsible for her post-Proposition 227 experience. The move to English Only was a policy enabler for Connie because she took personal and professional satisfaction from the move away from bilingual education. At the same time, the way in which the Open Court program was being implemented was a policy disabler because Connie felt she had little professional control of her classroom. Both of these realities ultimately influenced the local enactment of policy for Connie and her students.

Policy Enabler: "English should be the language of this country." The way Connie viewed and interacted with the decision-making structures in the school seemed to be in part related to who she was as a teacher and her feelings about the role English should play for her immigrant students. Prior to Proposition 227, Connie was classified as a "bilingual teacher," but she never recalls intentionally choosing bilingual education as her career path:

> Basically I fell into it. I have a lot of background in other languages, I enjoy that. My first year here eleven years ago I was assigned to a bilingual class not even knowing until I got my class list. That's how it was, I wasn't asked, I was just put in. (Connie, Interview, PH #2)

Her unintentional entry into the field was coupled with a striking agreement with much of the social discourse surrounding both the English Only and anti-bilingual education movements. In an interview, Connie commented, "I totally agree that English should be **the** language of this country. You need to have some base and I think English needs to be the base here." Connie believed that for her students to be able to succeed in America, mastery of English was paramount.

Her beliefs about language and the best way for her students to learn language were mirrored in the school. Connie participated in a planning group that was a subset of second grade teachers who met to plan Open Court activities for two-week blocks. These meetings offered little talk about the potential special needs of EL students and almost exclusively centered on how the teachers could maintain the coverage quotas set up by the Open Court Experts. Connie explained the meetings this way:

> We only do Open Court. There is one other ELD teacher. Out of the five there are two of us in there. But we go through planning the lesson. The other ELD teacher and I have to go back and adapt things on our own...The other three teachers basically don't have experience with the ELD kids at all. So, the ELD teacher and I have to go back to our own rooms and do it on our own. (Connie, Interview, PH #2).

In planning meetings that I observed, Connie's assessment of the lack of conversations surrounding the ELL students was accurate. These conversations were non-existent.

This reality speaks to the enabling situation in which Connie found herself. Connie was never a fan of the school's bilingual program nor a fan of bilingual education in general. Connie believed that her students would experience success if they stopped speaking Spanish in the classroom. Given her views about student learning and the role English should play in their lives, it was not surprising that Connie did not act to create spaces for ELD issues to be aired in the meetings.

When Connie did raise issues related to her students at school meetings, the comments generally related to "deficits" in the students. For example, during a second grade team meeting at which teachers discussed the qualities of and possible remedies for "at-risk" students, the entire discussion occurred without any mention of issues related to second language development. Connie did make one comment in this particular meeting, a comment regarding the lack of "home support" of her students and its relation to their poor performance.

The Open Court Grant as a Policy Disabler. Although Connie's experience of the move to English Only unfolded in a personally and professionally enabling context, the implementation of the Open Court grant was a policy disabler for Connie. Although she may have felt ideologically empowered by the move to English Only, she felt stripped of power in terms of her own classroom decision making. Connie resented her loss of control over the pace at which she was to cover the Open Court lessons and freedom to decide the grade level of curriculum she would use.

At the beginning of the year, the ELL teachers were given latitude by the principal in determining the grade level curriculum used in class. Connie choose to begin with the end of first grade curriculum for her third grade. For Connie, the choice was obvious considering what she viewed as the "lack of basic skills" of her students. By the end of the first instructional quarter, the principal, at the suggestion of the Open Court Experts, decided that all teachers would move to grade level appropriate curriculum. This was a huge source of controversy for Connie, who feared that her students would experience more failure and more frustration than she felt they were already experiencing with the first-grade curriculum. She expressed this sentiment in an interview shortly before the changes were to take place:

> I don't like that I am being pushed to move through the books so fast—and especially with this new pacing schedule that we have, our whole group is going to have to stay together and with my ELD kids—my kids have to stay at the same pace! Just because you pushed them though all the material does not mean they understood it...but there's a lot of things in the that program that I don't think my kids need right now. They need some basic things and I'm being told I can't do that. I have to push ahead. (Connie, Interview, PH #1)

Connie attempted to address these changes through several channels, but realized that ultimately the structure of the school and the grant left her little room to control the pacing of instruction and grade level of curriculum she wanted to use.

When considering the influence the school's literacy coaches and Open Court Experts had on her instruction, she said, "I feel like a little puppet who tries to do exactly how I'm told to do. If that doesn't work I can go back to my coaches and I can tell them, but they've never come back and told me a way to fix the problem." Implicit in Connie's answer was a sense of powerlessness she felt in her own classroom. Like Celia, she felt her door was always open and to that end was careful not to stray from the pacing and instructional arrangements of the Open Court Experts.

Connie was eventually forced to move to the end of second grade Open Court curriculum. Pacing and control of her classroom represented a major source of her agency in meetings with her colleagues and her literacy coach at the school. Her fear of the Open Court Experts as outside authorities "with a lot of power" limited her from ever confronting the Open Court Experts directly about this. Her actions consistently centered around making the case that she needed more time to do the activities in the Open Court units and that her students were not benefiting from being compared to the other students. This pattern unfolded in a planning meeting I observed in February:

> The five teachers on Connie's planning team have met to determine the exact shape of the lessons for the next two instructional weeks. Because the program is very regimented, most of this conversation centers around spending 3 or 4 days on a story and is then followed by a great deal of sarcasm

regarding how much "freedom" the planning team has.
Toward the end of the meeting one of the school's literacy
coaches walks into the room. Connie and another teacher ask
the coach several questions regarding the pacing schedule. In a
frustrated tone Connie expressed that "with a quarter of her
students qualifying for resource" (special education) she felt
the pacing was truly impossible. The other teacher actively
involved in the discussion expressed that she was "so
frustrated" by the pressure.

The coach responded in very carefully pronounced, almost
drawn-out words, "I think the pacing is fast. But the research
says that it is the amount of material that you cover not the in-
depthness in which you cover it that raises scores."

Connie shook her head, "I don't know. I have a real problem
with that. I feel to teach them well I need more depth."
(Planning Meeting, PH # 2)

Like most meetings related to Open Court, there was little Connie
could do beyond voice her frustrations about the situation. Throughout
the year, Connie commented that she was concerned that this
frustration showed up in her day-to-day interactions with her students.

Implication of Connie's experience. Although Connie welcomed
the school's programmatic response to Proposition 227, she deeply
resented the way Open Court was being implemented at the school.
Much like the teachers of Lortie's (1975) research, Connie wanted to
shut her door and be left alone, but the nature of Open Court
implementation prevented this from occurring. For Connie, being
ideologically empowered by the direction of the school towards English
Only clashed with the loss of control over her own classroom. In the
tension and negotiation of that space was where policy met practice for
Connie and her students. The result was that Connie felt empowered to
enact prohibitions against speaking Spanish in her classroom, but felt
unable to create a classroom environment she felt was appropriate for
her students.

Summary: Proposition 227 at Westway

The preceding discussion of Celia and Connie is designed to highlight how the district and school decisions regarding Proposition 227 impeded and created certain types of agency for teachers. Past research on policy has centered on the teacher as a conductor of new mandates (Darling-Hammond, 1990). For Celia and Connie, the policy mandates of Proposition 227 were not so much "conducted" as they were "experienced." Through their actions and experience of the new policy context created by Proposition 227, the teachers established a professional context for action. Through their work in English Only and Open Court, Celia and Connie experienced features of the new policy context that facilitated their taking action around particular issues. Certain aspects of the new context—particularly working with the Open Court experts—were policy disablers. Both Celia and Connie felt that working with the grant limited the types of professional freedoms and independent decisions they were able to make. At the same time, there were features of the new policy context that created room for Celia and Connie to act along lines with which they felt comfortable and that were consistent with their beliefs about the education of their students. Their experience of the new policy context created by Proposition 227 indicated that teachers' actions were mediated by the decision-making structures at the school.

Because Celia and Connie were different people with different individual characteristics, their experiences of the features of the new policy context were quite distinct. While they may have experienced the same features of the new policy context, the actions they elected to take or not take in that context were related to who they were as individual teachers. For Celia, the experience of Open Court and English only were a call to action. With her colleagues, her principal, and other district personnel, Celia raised issues she felt were important for the education of ELs at her school site. While she was not able to make significant changes to the manner in which Westway educated ELs, her actions brought issues she felt were missing in the official discussions regarding the education of her students to the table.

Connie's experience of the decision-making structures at the school indicated how a teacher with different individual qualities—including, personal history and attitudes about language and immigration—could take different types of action in the same policy context. Because of her ideological orientation with English Only, Connie was able to behave in the school site in the way in which she felt comfortable. For example, while there were no school-wide rules prohibiting students from speaking Spanish, the climate and direction of the school allowed Connie to implement prohibitions against speaking Spanish in her classroom. Additionally, the features of context created by English Only had freed Connie from talking about and listening to issues related to her students' development of English. This feature of the new policy context allowed Connie to act in meetings in a manner consistent with her personal beliefs about the education of her students.

OPEN VALLEY: CHARTING THE COURSE FOR BILINGUAL EDUCATION

While the school-wide context at Westway was characterized by a lack of curricular freedom, the situation at Open Valley was quite different. Two major realties shaped the culture and decision-making structures at the school. First, Open Valley had become a conversion Charter School to avoid having to complete the waiver process during the second year of Proposition 227 implementation. Second, the overall climate of the school showed an overwhelming commitment to the goals of bilingual and multicultural education. As teachers experienced and worked within these features of the new context, certain types of actions became possible, others more difficult. The features that facilitated teacher action at Open Valley are called policy enablers. The features of context that impeded teacher action are called policy disablers. Teachers' experiences of these features of context and the end result of their actions were influenced by their individual qualities. Before I examine Angelica's and Elisa's perceptions of and behaviors within this structure, I will examine how the Charter and program's place in the district contributed to the organizational context of the school.

The Charter: Uncertainties of a New Direction. To avoid a second year of the waiver process, the teachers and administration of Open Valley applied for and received Charter status for their school. This move was supported by the district's Superintendent who had been "whispering Charter" to the members of the school community since the passage of Proposition 227. Although the Charter gave the school curricular freedom, in all other matters Open Valley was "legally and officially part of Walton Unified School District" (Open Valley Charter, 1999). The curricular freedom of the school was balanced against the feeling of being on new ground. The school's principal, "Helen Edwards," explained that the school was in the process of figuring out its exact direction:

> Because we're dependent on the district yet we have an independence, I feel like sometimes it's hard to figure out the boundaries between the district and the school. (Helen, Interview, PH #2)

These boundaries were continually being worked out and their nebulous roles in determining the overall decision-making structure at the school were evident at the first school-wide governance meeting. The group of teachers and parents who comprised the school governing council met to discuss their role in running the school. As they were determining who would run the meetings and the process for decision making, a reading coach at the school commented, "The whole reason for writing the Charter was to save the bilingual program. We did that. Now, I want to go beyond that. We are a Charter School." While there was widespread agreement by the other teachers in the room regarding this comment, there was a sense that "going beyond saving the bilingual program" was going to be an arduous process.

Although the direction of the Charter created some ambiguities for the teachers and principal, there was also a sense of optimism and excitement surrounding the new direction. This excitement had its roots in the Charter as a policy enabler for the members of the school community. The Charter created new spaces for members of the school community to take action to address the educational needs of their students. The language of the Charter was heavily steeped in a commitment to producing and maintaining a learning environment that supported bilingualism and biliteracy. Helen believed that "The Charter functions as a kind of contract, and what we said we were going to do in the Charter was what we needed to do." She noted that the Charter had given teachers much more responsibility in determining the nature of literacy instruction in their classrooms. While the school still used the district's textbook adoptions, the "decisions of how we use them is made by the teacher in the classroom consulting with me and our reading specialist" (Helen, Interview, PH # 2).

Ultimately, Helen believed that the freedom in the decision-making process had a very positive influence on how teachers saw themselves and their new instructional roles in the Charter:

> I think last year the teachers felt like they weren't being considered the professionals that they are and having the knowledge that they do because programs were given to them.
>
> They **had to do** certain things. They weren't allowed to use their professional judgment in the classroom and they weren't being treated as professionals. I think this year with the Charter in place there is more of a professional feel for them. They are able to use their judgement in the classroom. (Helen, Interview, PH #2)

These two realities—the ambiguities of the new arrangement and the freedom of the Charter—combined to create a school context that was governed by a tension. This tension was characterized by the insecurity of working in a new structure where the teachers were playing a large role in determining what this structure would ultimately look like.

A second defining characteristic of the school was related to its commitment to the goals of bilingual and multicultural education. The Charter read like a counter-narrative to the arguments presented in Proposition 227. In addition, the Charter explicitly called on members of the school community to work to maintain and build connections with Latino parents of the school. These commitments were expressed through a number of events including parent educational forums, parent literacy nights, and cultural events which facilitated and demonstrated the connections between the work of the teachers and the lives of the parents.

For the teachers at Open Valley, the school's commitments and priorities were not represented at the district level. Angelica explained it this way:

> The Charter has made me feel like the people in the district don't care about us. They wasted so much money at the beginning of the year buying Open Court knowing that we

> were fighting to keep our bilingual program, knowing that we
> needed money to buy our new bilingual program. And, they
> didn't bother....They could care less how we felt or what or
> needs were. (Angelica, Interview, PH # 1)

This sentiment was expressed by many of the teachers at the school and
was representative of the "stepchild" feeling that many of the teachers
had regarding their positions in the district. This feeling was the
general sentiment of the teachers despite the district's initial
Proposition 227 implementation plans that gave the school latitude to
go in its own direction. More than the freedom to chart their own
curricular path, the teachers at the school felt they wanted someone to
stand up for them at the district level—to champion their causes against
the people who made Proposition 227 happen.

The kinds of action and space for action that the two teachers in
this research—Elisa and Angelica—believed were possible in the
existing structural arrangement of the school were largely influenced by
their individual qualities as teachers. The way they viewed the
decision-making structures of the school and were positioned by them
depended on the realities of their classrooms and the kinds of personal
perspective and opinions they brought to those classrooms. For
Angelica, an ideological commitment to bilingual education combined
with a high degree of confidence in her own ability as a teacher
contributed to the nature of agency she exercised at the school. For
Elisa, concerns about the need for guidance in her classroom and the
"freedom of the Charter" created a situation in which she sought
guidance but was not sure where to get it. In Elisa's case, her own
pedagogical insecurities limited the kinds of agency she could take.

Angelica: Fighting for Bilingual Education

Two individual qualities influenced the way Angelica saw the structural
realities of Open Valley: her deep commitment to bilingual education
and her confidence in her own teaching expertise and ability. These two
qualities interacted to create the realities of how she was positioned by
the structure of the school and district where she worked and the types
of agency she exercised within this structure.

A Commitment to Primary Language Instruction. Angelica's commitment to primary language instruction grew out of her own educational experience and her ideological commitment to preserve her language and culture. For her, the rights of Latino parents to have their children educated in Spanish were unquestionable:

> When Proposition 227 was happening, I saw a lot of Mexicanos on the news that said: Yeah, we live in this country and tenemos que hablar en ingles [We have to speak English] and blah, blah, blah, whatever. (Her tone becomes very angry) Who are you to speak for somebody else? That's your opinion and maybe you don't want to be bilingual and maybe you fell in love with this culture and left your past behind. But there are many of us who don't want to leave our past behind. (Angelica, Interview, PH #2).

Angelica blamed "Latinos who were bent on acculturation for making 227 happen." She saw her role in the classroom and the school as central in ensuring that the wrong people were not given voice in matters regarding her students.

While Angelica was not above tinkering with her instructional strategies or applying new techniques gleaned from collogues, she had supreme confidence that she was an excellent teacher. Her feelings about her own practice were not rooted in arrogance, but were evident in the extremely high standards she held for herself and her students.

In the beginning of the year, Angelica identified four students who came to her class reading well below grade level. She told me that "no matter what it takes," the boys would all be reading well above grade level by the end of the year. They were. When Angelica spoke of their growth, there was little pride or celebration in her voice. There was just the candor of a women who was quite confident in her abilities and the way she decided to shape her classroom.

We Are Still Standing. Angelica's perception of the lack of district support for the school's bilingual program was perhaps the single most defining force in shaping the nature of her work at the school. Her views of the district were compounded by her thoughts about Open Valley's principal whom Angelica believed was trying her best but did not "have it in her heart to go and fight" for the program.

Angelica believed that, for the bilingual program to succeed in a district where only one school maintained a bilingual program, Helen needed to be a strong advocate for the needs of the teachers and students in the program. Angelica's perception of Helen's inability to be that advocate created a situation where Angelica took an oppositional stance toward the district and "bought out" of many district professional development events. For example, she intentionally avoided meetings when possible. In an interview, Angelica explained:

> I know this job has been really hard for Helen. She has tried to do many good things for the school, but I think she doesn't know how.
>
> [Pretending to speak to Helen] If you really believe in the program and in bilingual education, then go crazy and go out and although people say, "No, you can't get this." You ask, you ask, and you ask. But now its like.
>
> [Pretending to speak for Helen] Okay you guys want to try this? I will present it. The district said no, you can't do this. Remember, we are under the Charter and we said we are going to be with our district. We get our funding from the district, so you guys have to go to those Open Court meetings even though you're not teaching it.
>
> [Speaking as herself] I made the choice. I'm not going to waste my time. (Angelica, Interview, PH 1)

Feeling that neither her principal or her district would take up the fight, Angelica took up the fight on her own. For example, she attempted to change the District testing schedule to administer the SABE 2 before the SAT 9. Angelica believed that a bilingual program should first test its students in Spanish and then English—to do otherwise misrepresented the priorities of the program. Angelica made several calls and visits to the district office regarding the feasibility of this plan as well as attempts to convince Helen that this move would be much better for the students.

Although she was unsuccessful at changing the scheduling of testing, her actions in the matter were illustrative of how a policy enabler created space for teacher action. The features of the policy context—the program's place in the district and Open Valley's principal's stance toward that place—served as a call to action. When her commitment to bilingual education met with the structural realities of the school, the result was a context that facilitated teacher agency. Angelica's actions were influenced by her view that the struggle of Proposition 227 had in some ways strengthened bilingual education:

> Proposition 227 pushed the people that did believe in continuing fighting for our dream. It's like a soccer game. You didn't make the goal. Oh, well. There's still team players out there in the soccer field. No todos estan derrotados [We are not all defeated]. You have the chance of getting up and trying again. Soccer players fall many times during a game. Kick the ball, trip over one and another. **We** can trip over these policies and fall over these laws. You can trip me and I'll fall, but I'm going to get up again. I'll keep going. And, when things like 227 or things like with this district happen—just don't trip and fall and stay laying down.
>
> I think people like the teachers at this school need to work together and continue and continue no matter what people say. We have to get up. And, yes it hurts when you fall. Yes, it's painful and it's hard to go against the current but it can happen. If you believe in it, it can happen. (Angelica, Interview, PH # 2)

Angelica combined the belief that "it can happen" with her commitment to goals of bilingual education continually in her work at the school. She took opportunities small and large to make sure that someone was "speaking for bilingual education." In Student Study Team meetings which were designed to examine and develop academic support networks for students, Angelica was the voice of primary language instruction. She argued that children should always get a chance to show what they know in their primary language before any talk of special education referrals could come to the table. Angelica believed that by "getting involved you're going to get more for you, your parents, and your students."

In addition to this involvement surfacing in her Student Study Team, Angelica was active in many other aspects of the school's maintenance of the bilingual program. In the first year of Proposition 227 implementation, she played a central role in organizing the parent meeting in which the school secured the waivers, and later, she was very active in the development of the Charter.

The Uncharted Ground of the Charter. Angelica's experience of the newness of the Charter did not have a large impact on how she saw her role as a teacher. Like the school's principal, she acknowledged that the Charter did bring some new instability to the school, but she did not see this instability interfering with her mission in the classroom. Both her confidence in her own abilities and her collegial relations with the group of teachers with whom she worked limited the potential instability caused by the Charter.

Angelica maintained strong connections with the teachers above and below her in grade level. Before the start of the academic year, these teachers met with each other to discuss planning and student development issues. Angelica believed that such practice with her colleagues allowed them all to keep focus on the school-wide goals of bilingualism and biliteracy. She explained: "I work very closely with the kindergarten teacher and the first-grade teacher and even the third-grade teacher. We always talk to each other. 'These are the types of kids and these are their needs'" (Angelica, Interview, PH #1). This environment of collegiality assisted Angelica in making instructional decisions. For Angelica, these decisions directly connected to her instructional goals. She noted, "I am just not going to choose any activity because it is in the teacher's guide."

Angelica's comfort with her own instructional choices and her deeply held commitment to the goals of bilingual education worked to create a situation where she continually served as an advocate for the program. She extended this advocacy to her extensive work with the parents of her children and her involvement in coordinating and planning activities for parental literacy nights.

Fighting for Bilingual Education. Angelica's comparison of the fight over Proposition 227 and a soccer match reveals the way the new law influenced the nature of her work. For Angelica, Proposition 227 was not the end of bilingual education in her classroom. The law was just another obstacle that she was willing to work around to accomplish her goals as teacher. Angelica cast Proposition 227 as an attempt to take voice away from the Latino community. Her work increasing parent involvement at the school and her role as a bilingual advocate were responses to the law's intent. In summary, Angelica found places and spaces to act as an advocate and spokesperson for bilingual education. This position grew out of both who she was as a person and how she was situated within the school.

Elisa: Mas Rebelde Meets Instructional Insecurities

While Angelica continually looked for opportunities to tell the world how well the school was doing in its bilingual program, Elisa longed for opportunities to talk with a credible outside source who could resolve her difficulties in running the school's English transition program. Elisa's experience with the school decision-making structure and the instability of the Charter were influenced by her own insecurities and her self-admitted longing for guidance.

Elisa's third-grade classroom played a central role in the school's overall bilingual program. Native language instruction was the focus of grades K-2. Instruction in Kindergarten was generally conducted in Spanish with limited time devoted to English language development. In first grade, students spent 80% of instructional time in Spanish and 20% in English. In second grade, students spent 70% of instructional time in Spanish and 30% in English. Third grade was designated as the year that the bilingual students would become prepared to handle instruction completely in English, which came in the fourth grade.

The demands of creating an effective and viable transition program were primary in Elisa's work. The year before, Elisa had been teaching 5th grade, so running the transition program was an entirely new experience. Viewing these demands in conjunction with her individual qualities presents a full picture of how Elisa was positioned by the structural realities of the school and district, and what room her positioning created for her to act on the dilemmas that most shaped her professional life.

A Commitment to Making a Difference. While Elisa struggled with many of the pedagogical realities of her classroom, she did not struggle with her commitment to "wanting to make a difference." This goal was connected to her reasons for entering the field of teaching and her deliberate decision to work with Latino students. Her goals as a teacher were closely related to her childhood experiences with migrant agricultural work.

> The sun was coming out at five o'clock in the morning. I was there alone. There was nobody in the field. I was just left there and I was waiting for the people to get there. I was maybe fourteen or fifteen. I kept thinking: What I am going to do? I don't work to work in the fields for the rest of my life. That's actually what brought up me wanting to teach. It's like: I want to do something productive for my people—for the kids and parents who work in the fields because I saw how hard they work and they really didn't make any money. So, I wanted to make a difference. That's why I became a teacher. (Elisa, Interview, PH # 1)

Although Elisa's ideological and personal commitment to bilingual education ran deep, when these commitments met with her pedagogical insecurities and the structure of the school they offered her little direction in how to resolve the pedagogical dilemmas she faced. In this sense, features of the new policy context served as policy disablers for Elisa. Her experience of the new context created a situation in which she felt she had few outlets or avenues to take to address issues and dilemmas in her classroom.

Transition: "We don't have a clear idea." When I questioned Elisa in an interview about her goals for the children in English literacy, her response indicated how she was positioned by the Charter and her instructional confusion regarding transition issues. The newness of the Charter and decision-making structures in the school offered her little help in dealing with the question of English transition:

> I think it's the transition of being a charter school. I don't know if I should say "we" or if English transition is all my responsibility. We don't have a clear view of what a transition program is. Whose responsibility is it to develop this program? The reasons I say that is that since I started thinking about how I am going to get my kids ready for the fourth

grade, I keep asking and really nobody has an answer. Como que me cambian la conversacion [They change the subject] or they tell me: Here's this. Use this and shut up. That's how I feel. I have the packets that people have given me that says "transition" on the top but it's like: Okay, so what do I do? (Elisa, Interview, PH #1)

Similarly, the school-wide goals of "bilingual and biliteracy," which were outlined in the Charter and were for Angelica a sort of *cause cèlebre,* were for Elisa a source of frustration. Speaking of the overall goals of the school, she noted: "I was excited about it. But then I started this third grade transition and it didn't really happen. It hasn't really happened. Because there are not clear answers, and there's no plan" (Elisa, Interview, PH #1).

Although Elisa's personal experiences fell in line with the nature of the overall goals of the Open Valley Charter, her pedagogical task and her need for guidance left her with little room to exercise agency to address her situation. For Elisa, these new features of the policy context created by Proposition 227 served as a policy disabler. Within the Charter structure, she felt there were few people to turn to because as the third grade teacher, Elisa was the only person at the school who was responsible for transition. While the early primary teachers could commune about primary language development and early literacy, no other teacher at the school had the same responsibility that Elisa had.

Compounding this situation were Elisa's feelings about Helen as the leader of the school. Although Helen had offered Elisa advice regarding the transition program, Elisa did not perceive Helen as a credible source of instructional support. This was related to Elisa's doubts about Helen's ability to lead a school committed to bilingualism and biliteracy. This situation created incredible insecurity for Elisa as she attempted to deal with the dicey and complicated issues of second language development: "I really don't know how much English I can give the kids without really taking away from their Spanish" (Elisa, Interview, PH # 2). Elisa asserted that some of this difficulty was probably related to her own difficulties understanding the "process on how kids learn" (PH #2, Interview).

Although she felt a great deal of pedagogical insecurity about what to do in her classroom, she did not feel comfortable turning to Helen for advice. Part of her lack of comfort level with Helen was related to

Elisa's reasons for becoming a teacher. Although she was not confident in her expertise regarding transition issues, she did not doubt her commitment to making life better for Latino students. She doubted if Helen shared the same commitment, and consequently did not see her as a viable person to ask for advice. Elisa also attempted to seek help at the English Language Advisory Committee meetings, but felt like she was chided by her peers for airing the school's dirty laundry in such a public district forum. This situation created a reality that governed how Elisa saw herself within the school structure and what she thought she was able to do within it—very little. Elisa wanted "somebody from the outside to come and really tell us what a good bilingual program looks like" (Elisa, Interview, PH # 2). Eventually, but very late in the year in her mind, Elisa took that feeling of paralysis and began to create an instructional course she was proud of, but by her own admission she felt this change had occurred way too late—she did not get the final version of the program going until March (a full discussion of this occurs in chapter 5).

Vigilant Language Keeper. While part of Elisa's experience of the new policy context limited the types of agency she could take, her experience of the school's struggle to maintain its bilingual program worked to make her a more vigilant defender of her language and culture. In this sense, the school's development of the Charter and the passage of Proposition 227 were policy enablers. Elisa's experience of these features of the context created space for her to be more committed to the ideological goals of primary language instruction. In an interview she explained:

Creo que me hizo un poco mas rebelde acerca de mi lenguaje, porque antes estaba like no debo hablar enspañol, no debo de hablar esto, debo de hablar ingles porque estan hablando ingles.

[I think it has made me a little more rebellious about my language because before I was like I shouldn't speak in Spanish and I should say that, I should speak in English because they are speaking English]. (Elisa, Interview, PH # 2)

Her renewed commitment to her language and culture was partly due to her experience of the environment at Open Valley, partly due to her experience in her post-Proposition 227 classroom, and partly due to the district's Superintendent, whom she considered a positive role model. The Superintendent spoke fluent Spanish and frequently spoke to the teachers in Spanish.

Individual Qualities Making a Difference. Although Elisa worked in the same organizational context as Angelica, her experience and perception of this context indicates the role teachers' individual qualities play in the policy implementation process. For Elisa, the school's direction in post-Proposition 227 was a source of pride and ideological empowerment. She did feel reinvigorated as a "language keeper," but this ideological enabler was balanced against the pedagogically disabling feeling she felt from working in the new policy context. This reality seemed to limit the types of agency and action she took. While Angelica used the school's response to Proposition 227 as a springboard, Elisa—perhaps a bit overwhelmed—felt moments of paralysis and confusion. In summary, Proposition 227 and the school's response to the new law worked differently for the two teachers.

TEACHER ACTIONS IN THE NEW POLICY CONTEXT

Past conceptions of teachers' roles in the policy implementation process saw teachers chiefly as "conductors" of policy mandates. As the experiences of the four teachers in this study indicate, teachers were not just conduits for the policy demands of Proposition 227. Teachers experienced policy. Their experiences were shaped by the features of the policy context created by Proposition 227 implementation. Policy enablers—moments when teachers felt they could take action—and, policy disablers—moments when teacher action was impeded—were features of the new policy context. Teachers, through their actions in the new context, shaped how the policy was experienced.

In this case, the complete experience of Proposition 227 implementation was created through dynamic interactions between what the district and schools decided about Proposition 227 and the teachers' actions vis-à-vis those decisions. Teachers' actions were mediated by the overall structures at the school sites. For example, Celia's attempts to change the nature of instruction for her students was a direct response to Westway's implementation of Proposition 227. Her attempts at exercising agency were limited by the use of English Only and Open Court at the school. Angelica's role as a bilingual activist was in direct response to features of the new policy context—namely, the marginal place she felt Open Valley's bilingual program held in the district. The experiences of the four teachers in their respective schools and work situations were part of the complicated and multilayered web of events that continued the Proposition 227 experience.

Because the four women portrayed in this research were four unique women, their individual qualities played large roles in their experiences of the new features of the policy context. At Westway, working under English Only was a structural feature of Proposition 227 experienced differently by Celia and Connie. For Celia, the situation resulted in her attempts to exercise agency by raising key instructional issues facing her students in school-wide discussions. For Connie, the situation resulted in her creating rules against the use of Spanish in her classroom. Both teachers took action in the new policy context, but the results and direction of their actions were influenced by who they were as teachers.

The roles that individual qualities played in teachers experiencing the features of the policy context were also at work at Open Valley. While Elisa and Angelica both had personal experiences that caused them to choose to enter the field of bilingual education intentionally, their experiences of the structures within their schools and their positioning by the decisions were quite different. Other characteristics—in this case perceived expertise as well as teaching context—came into play. The examples of the four teachers indicate that teachers—through their work in and out of classroom contexts—helped define how Proposition 227 was experienced.

CHAPTER 5

Proposition 227 and Teachers' Work: English-Only and Open Court

In this chapter, I address the connections between Celia and Connie's experience of Proposition 227 decision-making processes at Westway and their enactment of literacy practice. I consider the classroom practice of each teacher in a separate section. In each section, I address the structure of literacy instruction and the nature of language use within that structure. I conclude each section by addressing the connections of a teacher's individual qualities and the local enactment of practice in her classroom.

LEARNING TO READ AND LEARNING ENGLISH IN CELIA'S CLASSROOM

> The other first grade teacher has been really stressed out. All the Open Court People want us to do is teach reading. I am like, "Mija don't worry about it. Just do the best you can because the kids have got to learn the language before they can even read this stuff." (Celia, October 12, 1999)

Literacy instruction in Celia's classroom reflected the way she was positioned by the implementation of Proposition 227 at the district and school. For Celia, the implementation decisions were a source of professional and personal tension (see Chapter 4 for a full discussion). The tension this positioning created in her instruction was exacerbated

by the nature of Open Court, the school's literacy series, and the way
the school chose to use that series.

Apart from the hour that the first- and second-grade English
Language Development class spent in math instruction, the entire
instructional day was spent at what Celia called "doing Open Court."
Doing Open Court was not an unproblematic proposition for Celia. It
was full of tensions, conflicts and struggles, highlighted by her feelings
about the instructional needs of the students, her beliefs about the
benefits of primary language instruction, and the way the program and
key actors within the school worked to implement the program. As her
opening comment indicated, the goals of teaching reading and learning
English were not always complementary. Often, learning reading as
defined by Open Court and issues related to second language
development of the 20 students interacted in unforeseen ways to create
dilemmas for Celia. The following incident involving a whole class
activity designed to build the students' phonemic awareness
highlighted this tension.

> The students of Celia's class sit on the rug as she holds the
> thick spiral bound Open Court teacher's guide. The bubbly
> enthusiasm in her voice is mitigated by her careful and
> deliberate pronunciation of the words, "OK, we're going to
> play a game. I am going to read some words that all start with
> the same letter, and you are going to help me finish the
> sentence with words that begin with the same letter. OK, are
> you ready?"

> She scans the rug area and reads from the teacher's guide. Her
> pronunciation becomes more marked, "Bob's basket of
> berries." She pauses for a moment, "Can anyone give me
> another B word?" Anna immediately raises her hand, "B B."[2]

> "OK," Celia replies, "B B-ies. Alright Bob's basket of berries
> and B B-ies. How about another word, Luis?"

> Luis answers, "Berries."

---

[2] A capital letter standing alone (e.g. B) indicates the speakers said the
name of the letter.

"Mijo, ya tenemos berries [we already have berries], I need a B-word para aggregar este oracion. I need another B word to make the sentence longer. Something that begins with B that I can put in a basket." As she explains the activity to the student several student give her blank looks and there is a two second silence after she stops her explanation. She writes "B" on the board and there is still no response from her students. In the moments that followed the silence, Celia dropped this activity and continued working with the students on another component of the Open Court program. (October 18, 1999)

Like all activities in Celia's classroom, this one had an officially defined purpose. The structural arrangements at the school—observations by Open Court experts, observations by school literacy coaches, and Open Court meetings—worked to ensure that Celia was positioned to execute the purpose. Often, the official purpose of the activity and Celia's students' ability to participate in the official purpose were not a seamless fit.

The activity was a component of the Open Court Program's focus on "reading skills and fluency." The skill highlighted by the activity was phonemic awareness described in the Open Court guide as "essential to the children's progression to phonics and reading." Reading skills—such as phonemic awareness—were to be "taught explicitly and systematically." Instruction in this area was characterized as "sequenced, attentive to individual needs, and includes a great deal of relevant practice with engaging yet predictable reading materials" (Open Court Teachers Guide, p. 35F). Because the literacy program considered phonemic awareness as "listening to and reproducing sounds," in the eyes of the Open Court program as well as the school's literacy coaches minimal adaptation was necessary for Celia's students to participate in the activity. This view was communicated to Celia during the many Open Court meetings as well as one-on-one post-observation conferences.

The nature of student participation in this activity and Celia's attempt to facilitate her student's participation through her use of Spanish indicated that there may have been some truth to her claim that her students, who were in the initial stages of their English development, "have got to learn the language before they can read this stuff." Both responses by Luis and Celia indicated that "listening to and reproducing sounds" might not be such a simple task. The activity occurred in a highly decontextualized manner. While she did little to address the relative contextual poverty of the activity, Celia did use Spanish in attempt to get the students to participate more fully in the activity. But even this did not work, and Celia—whose students were unable to participate in the activity—made the decision to move on to a new activity.

This glimpse of the classroom life illuminates the key questions that guide this investigation of policy-to-practice in Celia's classroom:

> How were language and literacy activities structured in the classroom?
> How were other classroom literacy events illustrative of the tensions present in this event?
> How did her use of Spanish to help negotiate these classroom tasks illuminate larger policy-and-practice based questions?
> What role did Celia's individual characteristics play in the enactment of literacy practice in the new policy context?

Before these questions are discussed in detail, I will more fully describe Celia's classroom, her students, and the school's literacy program.

Celia's Classroom. Celia taught in an English Development classroom, one of the school's three programs for EL students. The other two programs were Structured and Mainstream classrooms. Celia's classroom was originally designed to be a classroom of high functioning first graders and lower functioning second graders. Approximately 13 first graders and seven second graders comprised the class. Celia's energetic and gregarious personality surfaced in her interactions with her students in many ways. Although she had doubts about the use of Open Court with her students, she was constantly, in her own words, "pumping it up." Her demeanor in literacy interaction approximated an indefatigable aerobics instructor working with a group of reluctant and out of shape aerobics students. Her attempt to "pump it up" was more than just a result of her personality. By staying true to the demands of the Open Court Experts and her literacy coaches, Celia hoped to have some leverage in shaping the nature and use of Open

Court with the EL students at the school in the coming years. She felt
that if she did the program exactly as they described and it didn't work,
she might be given more room to "do things my way." This created a
tension for Celia between making a short term sacrifice regarding what
she believed was best for her students and influencing long term change
at the school.

But while the tensions played on Celia's mind as she acted both in
and out of the classroom, even when things were not going well, her
demeanor seldom drifted far from that perpetually bubbly person
pouring energy into her teaching. Her positive outlook unfolded in a
highly regimented and structured program that emphasized direct
instruction. Writing, reading, and speaking were tightly controlled
events that originated and ended with the teacher. In these literacy
activities, Celia used Spanish in many ways. She generally began
instructional activities in English, but when students struggled to
understand, Celia would use Spanish. Some of the uses of Spanish
included translations of English words, attempts to extend student
conversational turns, and getting students "hooked" into a particular
activity. In addition, a great deal of the social conversation with the
children occurred in Spanish.

Of the 20 students in her classroom, all spoke Spanish as a primary
language. During Phase 1 of this study, most of the students spoke to
each other in Spanish. During Phase 2, a few students, particularly a
group of first grade girls who were, according to Celia, "doing very
well," spoke a great deal of English in both official and unofficial
classroom events. With the exception of this group of high achieving
girls, the majority of the class spoke an even mix of English and
Spanish with each other and Celia in instructional situations. This claim
is based upon my observations of classroom events.

Celia's views about the achievement of her students paralleled the
student patterns of language use. By the end of Phase 2 of this study,
Celia felt that seven students were doing very well academically. She
believed an equal number of students were performing below grade
level. Several of the students in the latter group were second-grade
boys who struggled with the demands of the first-grade curriculum.

The physical arrangement of the room mirrored the curricular
arrangements. Most of the materials in the room were part of the Open
Court Program. A rug area—which was used for blending, read-aloud,
phonemic awareness activities, and reading from the anthology—was

the only place other than their desks where the students spent any significant time during literacy instruction. At their desks, arranged in clusters of four and oriented to the front of the room, students participated in a variety of activities including Activity Sheets, Reading/Writing Connection, and reading of the Step-by-Step books.

TENSIONS, REALITIES, AND CELIA'S INDIVIDUAL CHARACTERISTICS

> If it wasn't for me, I don't think this program would be working at all. I know there are classes where there are English Only teachers where it is not working. It won't work if the teacher doesn't take the time to explain things. Sure we have our teacher's manuals in our hands—our little experts—but most of the time it says pair them [students] up with role models [native speaking]. Well, I don't have role models. And, even if I did, I don't know if it would work. Honestly, I think it has a lot do with me. The extra stuff I do all day. (Celia, Interview, PH #1)

It was with a sense of irony that Celia reflected upon her classroom literacy practice and considered how her instructional adjustments influenced student outcomes in her classroom. She shared these perceptions with me with a smile on her face—a smile that revealed the nearly impossible task of finding time to do "extra stuff." For Celia, finding pedagogical space to do "extra stuff" was difficult given the lockstep approach the Open Court program took to literacy instruction, and the tightly controlled environment in which teachers were to implement the program.

In this section, I will examine two components of the Open Court literacy program, the Reading/Writing Connection and Anthology Reading, to explore issues related to Celia's attempt to make the program work in her classroom. Through examining practice-based examples of literacy instruction in Celia's classroom, I will detail the connection between Celia's individual qualities as a teacher and the influence of Proposition 227 on her literacy instruction. The tensions and difficulties present in Celia's negotiation and use of the Open Court program mirrored her own educational history. Additionally, the connection between policy and practice for Celia was closely connected with her beliefs and feelings about educational issues facing her students.

Reading/Writing Connection: "Getting Good Language from the Kids."

> The Reading/Writing Connection workbooks make the children aware of and comfortable with the connection between reading and writing. For the children, the workbooks provide a place to practice what they are learning about reading and writing across the year. (Open Court Teaching Manuel, 13 F)

The Reading/Writing Connection worksheets highlighted control-based reading and writing activities including copying words, choosing words from lists of five or six words to write under pictures or complete sentences, and unscrambling a handful of words to make sentences. The skills covered in the Reading/Writing Connection coordinated with the decoding and blending skills the class was practicing. As the class moved further along in the Story Anthology, the Reading/Writing Connection stressed slightly less controlled writing (e.g., students given a list of 12 words to describe a picture). Generally, Celia worked on one Reading/Writing Connection worksheet a day. The worksheets were considered an integral part of the English Language Development program by Celia, the school's literacy coaches, and the Open Court Experts. Celia's literacy coach described the activity as a way for Celia to "get really good language out of the kids."

Celia did worksheets on the overhead projector, leading students through a controlled word-by-word reading of each task on the worksheet. During Phase 2, student participation changed to a limited extent, with a group of six or seven students playing a more active role in reading. By and large, however, Celia's voice was the dominant feature during worksheet reading. In addition to a directed reading of the worksheets, Celia tightly controlled the writing portion of the worksheets. Students wrote one word or sound at a time, as directed by Celia.

"*It just doesn't happen like they say it should.*" Celia had a critical eye about the difference between the way the Open Court experts claimed the Reading/Writing Connection should unfold in her classroom, and the way the activity actually did. She felt uneasy about their insistence that the Reading/Writing Connection was an adequate substitute for ELD instruction. She said that although the students were supposed to be able to do the Reading/Writing connection on their own, their inability to do so caused her to use the activity primarily as a vocabulary building exercise. During many of the Reading/Writing Connections, Celia would ask the students what a particular word meant, and the students generally replied with a one word Spanish response.

Celia's experiences with the Reading/Writing Connection activity exemplified many of the tensions that characterized her work as a teacher at Westway. These tensions originated in the beliefs that the Open Court Experts and the school's literacy coaches held about how Celia's students should participate in the Open Court program. For Celia, the official version of events differed from the reality of her classroom. Although the official programmatic purpose of the Reading/Writing Connection was English language development, most of Celia's students needed to be micro-managed through the activity. Although the official purpose was to allow students to practice what they had learned about reading and writing, that practice occurred in an unidirectional participatory setting. Although the Open Court Experts and literacy coaches believed the activity needed only minimal adaptation, Celia's experience with it indicated student participation in the activity required extensive translation. The tension between the official version and Celia's view of classroom realities was a large factor in determining how literacy instruction was conducted in the room. Her attempts to get her students to be meaningful participants represents one way in which she was shaping the nature of the new policy context at her school.

As Celia dealt with these tensions, her students experienced them as enacted literacy practices in the classroom. The way these issues interacted was evident in an example taken from a Reading/Writing Connection that occurred during Phase 1.

Students were told in Spanish to open up their workbooks to page 71. which contained two pictures. Each picture was on the side of a box. The boxes were filled with a handful of scrambled words. The first picture was of a turtle on what looked like a stage. The words in the box where:

has   girl a

The turtle little

Underneath the box of words was a set of three lines on which students were to write the unscrambled sentence. Celia said to the children, "Recuerden la tarea que mandè a la casa en lunes [Do you remember the homework that I sent home on Monday]? Remember it was a mix of words and you had to put them back in order." Then very encouragingly she said, "I bet you all know what we are going to do now."

Celia asked the students what they saw in the picture. Olga raised her hand and was called on. She said, "A turtle." Luis, who was not called on, called out "frog."

After asking the students a few more questions about the picture, Celia said 'I'm going to write the first word of the sentence. Do we see a word with a capital letter?"

Olga and Luis call out "The." Celia writes the word "The" on the first line of the worksheet and puts a line through it. She reminds students not to pick up their pencils. She writes a " 1" over "has," a "2" over "girl," a "3" over "a," a "4" over "turtle," and a "5" over "little." She asks the students what word they think says girl.

She asks them to tell her the number. A couple of students call out "number 2." She then circles the word girl on the worksheet. She tells the students they can pick up their pencils and write "The girl."

She walks around the room looking at students as they write on their worksheets. As she walks around the room, she says, "I want to hear you say girl as your write it. She sounds out "g" and "ir" several times as she is walking around the room. She tells the students that their "G" should look like the way she has written it on the board and that if their "G" does not look like hers or if it is not on the line (she draws an example of this on the whiteboard) that they should circle the letter and write the new letter above it.

[The class has finished the first problem and moved to the second]

Table 1 Celia Classroom Excerpt: He is doing eggs		
Celia	*Students*	*Action*
(enthusiastically) What do you see in this picture?		Celia is pointing at the first picture.
A bird and a tree. Can you make a whole sentence out of that? (This was addressed to Yasmin)	Gisela: A bird. Yasmin: A tree.	Gisela and Yasmin both call out without being officially recognized by Celia.
(Celia then looking at Yasmin and speaking very slowly) I see a bird (pausing for almost one second between words) in the…		Yasmin is quiet and does not respond to Celia's request.
What is the bird doing?	Luis: I see a bird. Jesus: He is doing eggs.	Luis calls out having not been called on. Jesus's hand is up and Celia nods in his direction.
(Celia looking directly at Jesus and encouragingly asks) Can you make a whole sentence out of that? The bird is laying (with emphasis on		

Table 1 Celia Classroom Excerpt: He is doing eggs		
Celia	*Students*	*Action*
"laying") eggs. Can you repeat that?		
	Jesus: The bird is laying eggs.	
OK, lets see here. What is the bird doing?		No response from the kids.
What I am doing right now?		Celia makes an exaggerated arm motion and mimes sitting.
	Ss: Sitting.	
That's right. The bird is sitting too. Let's look at the words.		

Until Jesus's comment that "he is doing eggs," the responses from the children were either one or two word utterances, or repetitions of what Celia has already said. More than anything else, this literacy event was defined by the confining nature of the official task at hand, a task that was limiting and not flexible. The one unsolicited bit of language that a child generated was Jesus' comments about the bird "doing eggs." But, because this was a fill in the blank activity in which "sitting in the nest" not "laying eggs" was the prescribed answer, Celia's hands were tied. In this case, although there was some flexibility in the talk surrounding the worksheet, what got written in the blank was non-negotiable. The energy of the interaction between teacher and student was directed at unscrambling the words. Given the systemic nature of the Open Court program, the words that were candidates for unscrambling were selected based on the sounds and spelling the students had been practicing.

Reading/Writing Connection: The Nature of Literacy Instruction. In Celia's classroom, the tension between what was supposed to be and what was had a major influence on the way students experienced literacy instruction. The Reading/Writing Connection was officially touted as serving the joint purpose of English Language Development and fostering student understanding of the connections between reading and writing. In the preceding example, the nature of interaction during the activity was determined by the rigid script Celia had to follow. The instructional script and the inflexibility of the task in the Reading/Writing Connection created a context in which students experienced literacy not as a social practice, but as a riddle that could be cracked with the help of an adult.

The "puzzle-like" nature of literacy instruction was evident in the way the first word was chosen to unscramble the sentence. Celia's clue to the children was not a meaning based comment, but a call for them to look for a word with a capital letter to put in the first position. Celia frequently made comments in literacy instruction that stressed grammatical conventions over meaning. In addition, students experienced writing as a tightly controlled activity. When students were given a chance to write, the emphasis was on "phonetic exactness"—how to represent sounds with letters. Literacy instruction based on such mechanical exercises left little room for active student participation. For Jesus, the participation structures of the activity partially invalidated his contribution. His suggested sentence did not fit in the pre-determined blanks. Such a context for literacy might lead students to conclude that there is little room for their interpretations and experiences in either reading or writing.

Celia was very conscious about the difference between the official definition of the Reading/Writing Connection activity and the way it unfolded in her classroom. Just as the tension in the activity was a major factor in determining the context of literacy instruction in the room, so too was Celia's awareness of this tension and her attempt to address it. Celia may not have agreed with the officially defined purpose of the event, but she indicated that she did want her students to be meaningful participants in the Reading/Writing Connection. Her goals were to "get them to talk" and to begin the process of independent writing.

Celia's views showed up in her attempt to contextualize the activity. She reminded the students that it was like activities that they had done in the past. During their writing of the first sentence, she told the students in Spanish that their parents were going to be very proud of how well they can write. Additionally, her excitement and enthusiasm about the original sentence produced by Jesus indicated that Celia was interested in attempting to find a place in the official curriculum for what her students had to say.

Celia attempted to create a space for her students' participation in the Open Court program. At times, the structure of the program as well as its implementation in the school limited the range of those curricular negotiations. During such moments, Celia would focus student attention on phonetic exactness. At other times, Celia managed to rise above the structure and center interaction on meaning. These tensions also played themselves out in reading instruction, which I will examine in the following section.

The Nature of Teacher-Student Interaction During Reading Events

As Celia looked back on the year and discussed the differences between the way the Open Court Experts viewed the Reading Anthology events and the way they unfolded in her classroom, she became very frustrated. The emphasis on coverage had created great pressure in her work at the school. She felt she had dedicated so much effort to stay on the pacing schedule that she had diverted energy away from serving her students. As she recalled how this pressure played itself out in her work with the students, she said, she "could have done better with the kids with some more support from somewhere else."

Her comments indicated that she was not entirely pleased with the curricular decision-making process at the school and how she was positioned by it. She dreamt of a different kind of support from "somewhere else," but beyond the Open Court Experts and the school's literacy coaches she had few other sources of support. Given that arrangement, Celia turned inward and drew upon her positive feelings about having a shared cultural and linguistic heritage with her students. Celia's classroom practice seemed to take shape in the space between the "support" she was receiving from the Open Court decision-making structure at the school and her own views and feelings about her Latino students.

A comment Celia made to me regarding her feelings that Proposition 227 could "work as long as the wrong people didn't dominate it" was indicative of her curricular struggle. She was positioned between a program and literacy coaches whom she at times saw as the "wrong people," and her mission and identity as Latina teacher. Interaction in reading events was representative of these tensions and consisted of six types:

> Spanish Translation/Word Meaning. Celia offered or solicited one word Spanish translations of words in stories.
>
> Phonetic Exactness. Comments that drew focus to decoding individual sounds of words.
>
> Events of Story Question. Questions soliciting retelling or summary of events from stories.
>
> Creating/building on Intertextuality. Comments or questions that drew upon past stories or instructional activities in which the students participated. Celia used these interactions to help students understand moments in the new stories.
>
> Concept Question. Questions that asked students to draw conclusions or make inferences about an event in a story. Or, extensions of story events to events in the lives of students.
>
> Turn Extension. Comment or question by Celia that facilitated students' turn at talk.

As the following event taken from a Phase 2 Anthology reading event indicates, the enacted nature of her literacy practice was not a smooth balancing act among the tensions she faced:

The students had just finished completing an activity at their desks in which they chose from three words to answer questions such as: Which is the stickiest? Glue, tuna, shampoo. The worksheet highlighted the sounds the class had been working on during blending. After the class had finished the worksheet, Celia told the group to, "Get your anthologies and go to the rug and open your book to page 54."

Celia made her way to the carpet area, opened her book to the story of the "The Hare and the Tortoise," and displayed the two-page story to her students. Several of the students struggled to find the story. Carmindo and Jesus (two students

Celia was most concerned about) flipped through their books randomly, looking up after each page they turned. She assisted the boys in finding the story.

After about a minute, she asked the students to raise their hands if they could read the title. She asked Jesus to read the title and he looked at the page for a moment. Tomas whispered in his ear and then pulled away. Celia said, "That's OK, you can help him." Tomas whispered into his ear and then Jesus said in a quiet voice "The Hare and the Tortoise."

Table 2 Celia Classroom Excerpt: Aseop Fables		
Celia	*Students*	*Actions*
We have talked about this before, raise your hand if you tell me what a hare is. Olga?		Olga's hand shoots into the air.
	Olga: Un conejo. [A rabbit]	
Un conejo, raise your hand if you can tell me what a tortoise is. Cathy?		Cathy, Lucia, Olga, Tomas and Maribel shoot their hands in the air when Celia says "raise."
	Cathy: Una tortuga.	
Una tortuga de tierra. Because he lives around the desert. And this story is a Aseop fable. Yesterday we read another story written by Aseop. What was the story that we read yesterday? Raise your hand if you can tell me what story we read yesterday. Tomas.		A group of students --Cathy, Lucia, Olga, Tomas and Maribel—listen very intently.

Luis, Carmindo, Jesus, and Fernando roll around on the floor. |
| | Tomas: The fox and | |

Table 2 Celia Classroom Excerpt: Aseop Fables		
Celia	*Students*	*Actions*
The fox and the grapes. OK, can you sum up this story of the fox and the grapes? Sara.	the grapes.	
The grapes	Sara: That fox. Because that fox went to the selva [jungle] and he want (pauses struggling for a word)	
Because they were sour. Did he taste the grapes? No forget it. (High pitch and fast pace) Did he keep trying?	Sara: Yea, and the fox say no I think no want grapes.	
Did the fox keep trying yesterday?	Ss: Yes. Group of engaged students: NO!	Student are quiet for a moment and then Celia shakes her head with a sort of stage exaggeration.
So let's read this story and see how we can connect this to our unit of To Keep Trying. OK, let's put our finger on the title. (In a warm and kind voice) No we were	Luis: The Fox, teacher?	Celia tilts her head and raises her brow.

Table 2 Celia Classroom Excerpt: Aseop Fables		
Celia	*Students*	*Actions*
reviewing the Fox and the Grapes, but we are going to start reading The Hare and the Tortoise. Follow with your finger. If you can read, I want you to (starts to whisper) whisper it. But I really want you to follow along.		(This story and Aseop fable were part a unit in the story anthology called "Keep Trying.") Luis looks up at Celia with a look of confusion.

Celia begins to read the story and the students hold their books in their laps. Three students do whisper the words along with Celia as she reads. Celia reads the text of the story in a very exaggerated tone with noticeable pauses between each of the words. During the reading, Luis and Fernando look at Celia with blank looks. Carmindo and Jesus move their lips and make some sounds mimicking the cadence of Celia's voice. The sounds they make are not words. As she reads through the story, Celia pauses her reading to pursue individual word meanings with the students and asks the students summative questions about the events of the story.

This reading event was situated between the "support" she received from the Open Court Experts and her own desire to keep all her students engaged. In this event, her attempt not to "lose the little guys" was pitted against the pressure from the Open Court Experts and literacy coaches to stay on the pacing schedule. As Celia attempted to facilitate her students' participation in the reading event, she was confronted with the reality that her students were not able to read the story on their own. Literacy instruction in the room and the nature of student participation in the reading event was not characterized by joint teacher-student participation. During the reading of the story, Celia seemed to be left with little choice other than to read the story and allow the handful of students who were able to participate in a meaningful way to do so.

Although the nature of student participation during the reading of "The Tortoise and the Hare" represented one of the many times during classroom instruction when only a few students and Celia participated, Celia attempted to make a wide space for student participation in the pre-reading discussion. Consider Jesus and Luis who both had trouble finding the story in the anthology. Celia made space for a more competent student, Tomas, to help Jesus read the title. Celia believed that, by using Spanish at the start of an activity, she could ensure that all of her students knew what was going on. She used Spanish to stress the concept that a tortoise was a type of land turtle—a distinction central to the meaning of the story.

Celia attempted to set the context of the reading activity by drawing on the students' past experiences in reading. In addition, Celia showed a willingness to let students have extended turns when they were summarizing the previous story. When Celia supplied the word "grapes" to Sara, Sara was able to continue her turn and offer a complete summary of "The Fox and the Grapes."

This reading event represented the many contradictions and dilemmas Celia faced. While she attempted to create an instructional context in which her students could be meaningful participants, such attempts took a great deal of time. In the curricular arrangements at the school, time was not something Celia felt she had. While she attempted to create opportunities for extended student talk, she was constantly struggling to keep her students' attention.

Selected Student Participation. During the actual reading of the story, Celia spent a great deal of time pursuing the meaning of individual words. She believed that the extent to which she had to do this interfered with the flow of reading, but felt she had little choice given her students' command of English. In addition to going over word meanings, Celia spent time asking scripted questions that were closely connected to the events of the story. In my analysis of the reading events, the scripted questions were found to be closed-ended queries with limited possible one- or two-word answers. Scripted questions were a sub-code of the "Events of a Story" code. Scripted questions constituted the majority of question types in both the Anthology reading events and the Step-by-Step book reading events.

When the focus of teacher-led discussions was on a concept in a story, very few students participated. The following discussion that occurred after the students had finished reading "The Tortoise and the Hare" was illustrative of this pattern:

Table 3 Celia Classroom Excerpt: Hare and Tortoise		
Celia	*Students*	*Actions*
Who can sum up what happened in this fable? Cathy.		Cathy raises hand.
The hare wanted to beat the who?	Cathy: The hare want to beat him.	
And what happened at the end, who won the race?	Tomas: Tortoise Cathy: He wanted to win the race.	
The hare won the race? Raise your hand if you think the hare won the race.	Cathy: The hare.	Her response is echoed by a few other students.
		About half the class raises their hands.

She explains that the tortoise won the race. She asks the students to raise their hands if they can tell her why the tortoise won the race. Carmindo and Luis chat in the corner of the room. Celia repeats the question and calls on Olga who raises her hand.

She says, "The rabbit um, um, because the rabbit was sleeping and the tortoise was walking and then the tortoise um um won the race."

Celia asks, "Did the tortoise ever stop?"

A few students call out, "No." Celia stops this discussion to reprimand Luis who had his back turned to Celia and had begun to talk to Fernando. She told the class, "That's right sometimes when you're not the best at something and you try and try and try you can get something done. It is a very big word.

It's called perseverance. If you try and try. Did the turtle try, try and try?"

There is no response from the class.

With one exception, each of the questions that Celia asked the students focused on events in the story. The "event questions" had one or two word scripted responses. The one question Celia asked that focused on a concept of the story (why the tortoise won) was answered by Olga—one of the handful of students who Celia felt was doing very well in class. Although there were discussions in the class that focused on concepts, the number of students who could participate in those discussions was limited to a select few. During such discussions, a sizable portion of the class was engaged in disruptive behavior and was essentially tuned out of the discussion.

While the coding of reading events indicated that the nature of teacher-student interaction focused on word meaning and events of the story, the analysis also showed examples of Celia's attempts to make sure the "wrong people" did not always determine what unfolded in her classroom. Celia emerged as an energetic and compassionate teacher who tried to make her room a humane place for her students. Her use of Spanish and her attempts to facilitate student participation indicated that Celia's implementation of Open Court would make room for the needs of her students.

Spanish Read-a-Loud: Changing the Learning Context. While many of Celia's attempts to facilitate student participation in her classroom were subtle (an attempt at turn extension, a quick English translation), not all of Celia's instructional practice was characterized by piecemeal adjustments. Celia's use of Spanish read-a-loud during the 10 minutes of story read-a-loud time allotted by the pacing schedule was indicative of how her individual qualities informed her practice. The Spanish read-a-loud event also illuminated how changes in the context of an activity, in this case the language of the story, could drastically alter the participation patterns of students:

Celia holds up two books, one in Spanish and one in English. She tells the students, who are all sitting on the rug, that they are going to take a vote to decide which one they are going to read. As she holds up the Spanish book, Jesus calls out in an angry tone, "This is boring."

Luis imitating Jesus' angry tone says, "I hate this."

Celia: What do you hate?

Jesus: Spanish.

Celia: (with a look of incredulity) ¿Què habla tu mama? [What does your mom speak?]

Jesus: (defiantly) Spanish.

Celia: Then you have to like it. You have to be proud of tu idioma [your language].

Celia was momentarily interrupted by a phone call, and then she began reading the book Agarrar la Luna to the class. The students were intently looking on as she read. Their eyes did not stray from the pages. As she turned the pages of the story they seemed to wait in a sort of suspended trance for the next line of the story. The story detailed two children and an elephant's use of a kite to reach the moon. Once they landed on the moon, their weight brought the moon crashing to earth. The story then deals with the children's attempts to get the moon back to its proper place in the sky.

Celia believed it was important to read to her students in Spanish to counter what she felt was the overall negative position of Spanish in the school. The comments made by Jesus and Luis indicated that the two boys had internalized much of this negative sentiment toward Spanish. Celia's response to the boys reminded them that language is what connects them to their families. While their negative comments regarding Spanish speak to the position of Spanish in the school, their participation in the Spanish reading event that followed those comments demonstrated how student participation can change when the context of an activity changes. During the reading of the story, the class had a discussion about whether the story was fantasy and fiction. The class spent several conversational turns discussing this topic. In addition, many of the students who were frequently not engaged in classroom events were active and eager participants in the discussion.

Table 4 Celia Classroom Excerpt: Fantasy or Fiction		
Celia	*Students*	*Actions*
From listening to the story do you think that it is fantasy or realistic fiction? How do you know this? Raise your hand and to tell me. How do you know that this story is fantasy? Erlinda.	[Five or six students] (including Jesus and Luis): Fantasy!	Celia stops reading the story. As she begins to speak in English, the pace of her words slow noticeably.
And can you go to the moon with the kite?	Erlinda: Because the elephants don't talk. Luis: Elephants donna talk. Ss: No. Jesus: Yo pensaba que no encuentran la luna?	Luis calls out. Although he speaks over Erlinda, it is not in a disruptive tone. His comments almost have the effect of stating his agreement with Erlinda. Jesus had tried to

Table 4 Celia Classroom Excerpt: Fantasy or Fiction		
Celia	*Students*	*Actions*
Well, let's find out.	[I thought that they were not going to find the moon.] Carmindo: Le van (al) cansar! [They will reach it!] Olga: (To Carmindo) Si. Si. [Yes, Yes.]	call out during the initial question but was talked over by Luis and Erlinda.

Student participation in this event was striking for several reasons. First, many students who seldom participated in classroom activities were active participants in this discussion. Their participation in these events extended beyond one word answers to closed-ended questions. Erlinda, Luis, Jesus, and Carmindo were part of a group of a students who generally spent more time disrupting class events than participating in them. In this case, the fact that the story was read in Spanish allowed them to participate in a discussion about a concept.

For Celia, reading the story in Spanish seemed to free her of the usual demands Open Court activities placed upon her. She did not have to translate each word of the story to get students to participate in answering questions. Additionally, the discussion showed a flexibility that was not characteristic of other class discussions. Not all conversation began and ended with Celia. In the final moments before they continued reading the story, Olga had a direct exchange with Carmindo. While this may not seem like a pedagogical miracle, in the general structure of Open Court such discussions were rare.

Individual Qualities of Celia and Classroom Practice

While several factors—including Celia's position within the school and district-level decisions regarding the implementation of Proposition 227—were responsible for the local enactment of Proposition 227 in her classroom, Celia's individual qualities as a teacher played a significant role in determining the connection between policy and practice. In many ways, the tensions that played themselves out in Celia's classroom were the same ones at work in Celia's own educational history. Celia's room was characterized by a compassionate stance toward the language needs of her students, but a willingness to give the English Language Development model adopted by her school a chance for the hope of effecting change in the future. While she was willing to adopt the instructional stance of "English Only" in the classroom, she still used some Spanish and continued to do Spanish read alouds. Her classroom context represented a sort of straddling of both worlds. Her reaction to Proposition 227 implementation and her own educational history represent a dichotomy as well. Speaking of her educational experience she said:

> I remember how I felt. I remember that feeling of not being able to communicate to the teacher. All the way up until the third grade, I can remember the teacher talking and not being able to understand what she was saying. I didn't learn how to read until I was in third grade because I didn't have enough English and I was never placed in a bilingual classroom. It was always immersion. Bilingual education was something new to me. Until I started college I had never heard of it. When people brought it up, I was like, "No, I don't think its necessary. I never needed it." (Celia, Interview, PH #1)

As she was discussing her entry into the field and her educational experience, she paused and wondered, if maybe bilingual education would have helped her, given how long it took her to learn to read. She wavered a second time and said:

> (Hesitating) Now that I think about it, I don't think I would have developed my English. Well, it took me awhile, it took me four years, but I didn't have anybody at home who spoke English. So maybe to a point it would have helped to develop my literacy a little bit better. Me as a person, I think it would have made me feel more successful. Because I remember being in the first grade the teacher couldn't provide the necessary information to me to tell me what was going on in

the class. She didn't speak any Spanish so she put me back in a corner with a video and an audio cassette listening to books. That is what I got for reading. I can remember that because she couldn't do for me because I didn't have the language. (Celia, Interview, PH # 1)

In many ways, Celia's interpretation of her educational experience highlighted the tensions that existed in her classroom. Celia's educational history was not a story that fit neatly into a pro-bilingual or pro-English Only mold. While it had been hard for her as a child, she succeeded nevertheless. She balanced this success against the stress and isolation she recalls feeling as a child.

The difficulties Celia faced as a student seemed to be the same concerns she addressed in her classroom. She believed English Only could work if the "wrong people didn't get a hold of it." Her local enactment of practice seemed to be a constant struggle against the dictates of the "wrong people." Her use of Spanish in the classroom seemed to be a direct response to the isolation she had felt as a child. Her adaptations of the Open Court program showed that local enactment of policy mirrored the educational experiences of the teacher in the room.

CONNIE: A DIFFERENT TEACHER, A DIFFERENT ENACTMENT OF PRACTICE

My students' problem is that they rely too much on their Spanish. I know a lot of them came from second grade classes where they spoke Spanish all the time to the teacher. It makes a big difference. My goal is that they learn as much vocabulary as they can, learn to speak grammatically correct, and have their adjectives and nouns in the right places. (Connie, Interview, PH # 1)

Connie's response to a question regarding her goals for her students and the difficulties she was having helping the students attain those goals reveals two of her beliefs: 1) Spanish was a detriment to her students' academic progress, and 2) what her students needed most were the "basics." In the sections that follow, I will further explicate how these two beliefs worked to create the nature of practice in her classroom.

Although her beliefs about the students' language use and their instructional needs shaped the nature of the instruction in this third-grade English Language Development Classroom, Connie's local enactment of policy was situated in the organizational decision-making structure of the district and school. Connie experienced the same structure of Open Court decision making as Celia. She was seen as a teacher in a school with an inadequate program prior to Proposition 227. By the district, she was seen as a teacher in a school without a deep commitment to bilingual education.

Although Connie and Celia were positioned within the decision-making structure of the district and school in similar ways, the manner in which Connie related to that organization was quite distinct. Her relation to the decision-making structures, her positioning, was dependent upon who she was as a teacher. Her individual qualities—her beliefs about her students' language and culture, her entry into the field of teaching, as well as her views on immigration—interacted with her organization in the school and contributed to the way she was positioned.

Connie felt her beliefs about the role a student's primary language should play in instruction were validated by Westway's shift to English Only. For Connie, the tensions in her work at the school existed not in what was being implemented, but how it was being implemented. Connie resented being cast as a "puppet" by the Open Court Experts. She resented knowing that "these people can just walk into our rooms whenever they want." Most of all, she resented being compared to her peers. For the Open Court Experts, it was crucial that all teachers execute the program in the same way and at the same pace. Given that Connie felt her students needed the basics above all else, she felt this was an unfair demand upon her work. Connie wished the school could "just have Open Court and lose the grant." She explained, "the pressure from the grant is just not healthy. We are all running around crazy. We're all upset and we take it out on the kids" (Connie, Interview, PH # 1).

Enactment of Practice

The local enactment of literacy instruction in Connie's room took shape between her beliefs about her students—that they needed to stop speaking Spanish and would most benefit from instruction centering on "the basics"—and the "pressure to conform" to the demands of the Open Court Experts. The result was a curriculum that stressed decoding skills over meaning. These realities are the highlighted in the following worksheet event:

> Connie stood at the front of the class and read the first problem of the worksheet. She instructed students that they were supposed to circle each long vowel sound in each of the sentences and write the word in the long vowel column. This was the third in a series of worksheets the class had done that day. Connie completed the first three sentences with the students. In each sentence, her pattern was fairly consistent. She read the sentence and asked the students which words in the sentence had a long vowel sound. Students were not allowed to pick up their pencils until the class had identified all the long vowel sounds. During the first three sentences, a few students called answers without being officially recognized. When this happened on the fourth sentence,
>
> Connie said, "Since you seem to have no problem with this activity you can do it on your own."
>
> Ruben and Miguel, who were seated on the opposite side of the room from where I was, excitedly rubbed their hands together. I got up from my seat and sat behind Miguel, a child who always seemed to have a smile on his face.
>
> Miguel: (Reading number 5) (Reads in a flat tone with no questioning intonation.) Will Pat go to the store. (Pauses for a moment) Will Pat **go to** the store. (Flat intonation). Will Pat...Pat go to the store? (An almost raised but unnatural intonation on store). [He raises his head from the text]. That doesn't make any sense. (almost smugly) Don't matter. [He

picks up his pencil and writes the words "go" and "store" in
the Long O column.]

This literacy event highlighted many of the themes that emerged from
the study of Connie's classroom. Classroom instruction focused on the
component parts of reading. Connie's comfort with this focus was
related to her views about the instructional needs of her students. The
event also highlighted the tightly controlled nature of literacy events. In
the activity—as was the case with many others—students were allowed
to do the work independently only as a form of punishment. Lastly, the
event indicated the nature of students' experiences of a literacy
curriculum that stressed skills over meaning. The event raises several
questions that will guide the discussion regarding policy-to-practice in
Connie's classroom:

> How were literacy events structured in the classroom?
> How did the teacher and students use language (Spanish
> and English) within these events?
> What did Connie conceive of as her main purpose in
> literacy instruction?
> What was the relationship between the structure of
> literacy instruction in the room and Connie's
> characteristics as a teacher?

In the follow sections, I will examine three types of events which
dominated the instructional day dictation, skill based worksheets, and
teacher directed reading. I will consider how these literacy events are
related to the way Connie was positioned at the school.

Connie's Classroom. Connie taught a third-grade English
Language Development classroom of 20 Latino students, nearly all of
whom were born in Mexico or had emigrated to the U.S. at a very
young age. Although many of these students spoke Spanish to each
other, Connie had clearly stated rules about the use of Spanish in her
classroom. She said, "I don't speak Spanish. I don't allow them to
speak Spanish unless they can't say it in English. That's not Open
Court. That's just my strong feelings about teaching" (Connie, PH # 1,
Interview). During my observations, Connie frequently reminded the
students of this rule. The refrain, "If I would have wanted it in Spanish,

I would have asked for it Spanish," was a common occurrence in her classroom. Connie did have some knowledge of Spanish. She reported to me that she could understand a great deal of what students and parents said, and could communicate in Spanish, if she had to.

The majority of literacy instruction occurred with students sitting at their desks. Connie frequently led the students through activities one question or task at a time. Students were not allowed to exceed the pace established by the teacher. During blending, students were warned not to read a part of the word unless Connie had actually pointed to it. During worksheet events, students were scolded for moving ahead of the group.

A typical day's events included blending, dictation, skills and phonics review worksheets, reading of the step by step books, and reading from the anthology. Literacy instruction occurred from 9:30 until the end of the day. While she lamented the absence of Social Studies and Science in the curriculum, Connie felt the nature of the grant and her students' needs left her no alternative than to devote the vast majority of her day to Open Court.

Connie acknowledged that the arrangement wore on both her and her students. This reality created a situation in which Connie frequently looked frustrated during classroom instruction. She felt this had been one of her most frustrating years in her ten-plus years at the school. This frustration appeared to contribute to her non-energetic demeanor.

The physical arrangement and lack of movement of the students mirrored the teacher-directed nature of instruction. Students sat in individual desks that were oriented towards the front of the room in a large U-shape. Occasionally students moved to the floor space for blending or reading exercises. The room was sparsely decorated. Most wall hangings were part of the Open Court Curriculum (sound spelling cards, Open Court word wall, etc).

THE NATURE OF THE BASICS

I think Open Court is really good when it comes to meeting the EL kids' needs and I really like the structure of the program—how it teaches all the sounds. Every things is really laid out, so if a child has a problem it can be addressed. If a child begins with the program in kindergarten or first grade, there is almost no way they couldn't learn to read. (Connie, Interview, PH #1)

Connie's affinity with Open Court was a contributing factor in the nature of instruction in her classroom. She viewed teaching the "sounds" of the English as the answer to all of her students' academic problems. A great deal of time was spend on "the sounds" and making sure that students said them with proper pronunciation and could replicate those sounds in writing. Connie felt this focus would address the most central needs of her students. Her desire to make sure her students learned the basics was rooted in her beliefs about the home environments of her students.

> The biggest thing I see with this year's group is a lack of basic school skills... Just basic common sense things that you learn in kindergarten that a lot of them are really lacking. Almost all of my students come from a home environment where—as often as I see non-academic home situations, a lot of these homes are more so. They're just—nothing. A lot of illiterate parents in this class. Education is just not a priority and the kids just don't have the basics they need to succeed. (Connie, Interview, PH #1)

To address these issues, Connie created a tightly controlled instructional environment. Teacher control permeated nearly all literacy events. Interestingly, the student experience of this control did not always support her beliefs about the instructional needs of her students. The student experience of a blending event that occurred during Phase 2 of the research indicated that "the basics" and the needs of her students were not always an identical match.

> The students are sitting at their desks and have just finished the first part of dictation. They have written six one-syllable words that highlighted the different spellings of the long-U sound. Students were not allowed to talk during dictation and were given one to three minutes to write a single word. Connie read the dictation word, used it in a sentence, and then spent a fair amount of time sounding it out—phoneme by phoneme. At times, she repeated a single phoneme eight times.

Table 5 Connie Classroom Excerpt: Challenge Word		
Connie	*Student*	*Action*
Challenge word, Oh my goodness.	S: No teacher S: No S: No teacher Roberto: Yes, teacher! Miguel: (Firmly to Roberto) No, teacher!	
Guys, please. OK, (raised voice) listen to the challenge word and then we will break it down. (Slowly saying the whole word) Parachute.		
Pa Pa OK, listen write Pa, pa, pa.	Anna: (overlapping Connie) Park, teacher?	Connie points to the "armadillo card" which is one of the Sound-Spelling cards on the wall. It is a vowel card and lists all the spellings of the English phoneme [ar].
You're listening. I am the only one talking. Pah Pah. Er Er. Look at your armadillo card. Er. Er. Er.		
	Carlos: (directly to Connie) The "U" teacher.	Students can be heard repeating the sounds.
Er ah ah. You should have four letters. Pa your armadillo. Para.		Connie is walking around the room. She stops to help Carlos.
	Carlos: Par "uh" "uh."	
(To Carlos) Go ah, I said ah, ah. Some people actually say		A few students mouth the sounds of the word.

Table 5 Connie Classroom Excerpt: Challenge Word		
Connie	*Student*	*Action*
para "uh" chute. I guess I say para ah chute.		Connie walks to the front of the room.
Chute, how am I going to write that? Look at your chipmunk card.

Chipmunk card... | Miguel: (Directly to Connie and pointing at the word in his dictation booklet) This is TH. | The "chipmunk card"—like the armadillo card--is a Sound-Spelling Card. The card has a picture of the animal and underneath it: ch _tch |
Chipmunk card is a TH?		
	Miguel: Yea, I mean or T C H.	
(Agitated) Chipmunk card. (Raised intonation) What's on the chipmunk card?	Roberto: *Hay* two (to himself). Miguel: (Pointing to card on the wall). CH or TCH.	Roberto is next to Miguel.
Well, listen to me parachute (w/emphasis). (Looks back at the card) I'll tell you it is the top spelling.

Para chuuute. You figure out the rest to get the long U. Shoot Shoot. "oo". Shoot" | Roberto: Oh. Miguel: Thank you, teacher.

Manuel: Shoot your foot? [confused] | |

Dictation was one of the major writing opportunities for the students in Connie's classroom. In this dictation event, teacher instructional discourse centered around phonetic exactness. This was a consistent pattern in the daily dictations. The individual words the class were to spell were treated as phonetic puzzles. The meaning of the word, the way it might be used, or its connections with the students' lives was seldom highlighted in these types of interactions. The phonemes of the word and ensuring that students combined those phonemes in the correct order were stressed.

During my observations, there was little indication that this emphasis on phonetic exactness or the treatment of text as puzzle aided the students in their attempt to make sense of written English. In fact, Miguel's struggle to correctly spelling the last syllable word "parachute" indicated that the teacher focus on phonetic exactness offered little help. While Connie attempted to aid the students in writing the word by referring to one of the sound spelling cards, the cards offered little help to Miguel. Miguel astutely pointed out that the card actually contained two possible spellings for the sound in the word. This was also highlighted by Roberto. He was only able to spell the word correctly when Connie identified which of the sounds finished the correct spelling. For Manuel, Connie's repetitions caused him to lose sight of the actual word the class was spelling.

Writing Events in Connie's Classroom

While dictation represents perhaps the most extreme example of an emphasis on phonetic exactness and teacher control, the pattern set by dictation filtered into other classroom worksheet events. During the second half of the year, the complete control that characterized worksheet events was eased. Connie allowed students to work more independently. While there was change in the control mechanisms of the class, the emphasis on phonetic exactness and skills was omnipresent. During these events, little explanation was offered as to why students were doing a particular exercise. For example, during the "Phonics Review" event I will describe, students were told they had to work really hard because "You've got a whole pile of these to do today."

In the following event, I concentrate on one dyadic encounter. Because Connie gave the students more time to work independently on the Phonics and Skill Review worksheets, one-on-one teacher/student interaction constituted one of the major instructional structures in the classroom. During these events, Connie walked through the room asking students questions and giving assistance. The nature of the questions and the assistance centered on three types of interactions: procedural questions, focus on phonetic exactness in the students' work, and task-driven questions. During procedural questions, Connie focused students' attention on the directions of the activity or following the procedures she had established during her brief framing of the activity. Teacher-run interactions centering on phonetic exactness were moments when emphasis was placed on the proper pronunciation of a word during student reading. In task-driven questions, Connie asked the students questions designed to assist them in completing the task of the activity.

In the following event, Connie's interaction with one student and her views about her become quite instructive in understanding the structure of literacy events in the classroom. The interaction occurred as Connie spoke to Patricia regarding the first problem on a Phonics Review Worksheet. Connie was very concerned about Patricia because of her apparent reliance on Spanish. Connie believed that because Patricia had recently come from a bilingual program in a neighboring district, "she needed a lot of extra support." Connie considered Patricia a very poor decoder, and placed her in the lowest ability group, which included three students Connie described as "pre-literate." The following interaction occurred after Connie had explained the activity of the Phonics Review worksheet:

All of the students in the class with the exception of Marco, David, Maricela, and Martin are working at their desks on the worksheet. Connie has sent these four students to work with the Spanish-speaking teacher's aide on the Phonics Review. Connie considered these four students her greatest concern. This group, which at times included Patricia, always spent a great deal of instructional time with one of the teaching aides who worked in the room.

Connie circles the room and has one- or two-turn exchanges with students. She has them read the words in the box or read the sentence to her. She approaches Patricia as she is working on a problem on the worksheet that reads: "Peg _____ a pink ribbon." The three words from which students could select to fill in the blank were cut, cue, clue.

C: OK, what is she going to do with the ribbon?
P: She is going to, uh...
C: (Pointing to the word cut in the box) What is this word?
P: Cut.
C: OK, Peg cut a pink ribbon. Does that makes sense? [Patricia scrunches her nose into a ball and raises her brow in a half "I'm thinking" half "I don't know posture."] Peg cut a pink ribbon, does that make sense? She has a long ribbon and then she is going to cut the ribbon?

P: She is going to cue it?
C: (slightly disappointed tone) You know what, you go ahead and go back there [C points to the table of students working with the aid] You need more help. You can stay over there.

Patricia picks up her worksheet and moves back to the table with the aide and four other students.

Like in the dictation event, teacher-student interaction in this event focused on treating the text as a puzzle. Patricia seemed to be confused by Connie's second rephrasing of the question, "She has a long ribbon and then she is going to cut the ribbon?" The interaction between Connie and Patricia was focused on filling in *one* word in *one* blank. Both Connie's tone and the nature of the task-driven questions had the effect of causing Patricia to search for a new word that would fit into the puzzle. Like the dictation event, the structure and context of instruction provided little space for the teacher to offer support beyond treating the text as a puzzle. The level of the teacher's instructional discourse never strayed outside the *one* sentence and the *one* blank. When Patricia was not able to meet the demands of filling in the blank, she was sent back to the work with the aide.

Understanding the significance of this event requires considering the types of questions Connie posed to Patricia and the end result of that process. The nature of the activities in the Open Court program and Connie's predilection towards deficit teaching created an instructional context that solely focused on filling in the blanks. This focus established patterns of participation for both Connie and the students. Interaction in this events centered around procedural questions, phonetic exactness, and task-based questions. When students were not able to "fill in the blanks," these types of questions constituted the major source of support offered by Connie. If Connie's support did not help students complete the assigned task, there seemed to be little instructional space left for Connie to address the students' needs.

In the event involving Patricia, Connie made the decision to send Patricia to the "low group" working with a bilingual aide. After Patricia's final comment, Connie concluded, "You know what, you go ahead and go back there [the back table with the low group]. You need more help. You can stay over there." In this case, "over there" was a group of students whom Connie often referred to as lost causes. Connie often spoke of the students in the "low group" in terms of exasperation that bordered on distaste. The four students in the group were her consistent behavior problems. Often during classroom activities, the students were sent out of the room or given low level work to complete while the class worked on other activities. Connie's decision to send Patricia to work with this group of students revealed how literacy instruction was experienced by the students in the room. When Patricia could not complete the answers of the worksheet in the structure of participation established by Connie, she was excluded from having further interaction with the teacher. Connie, having exhausted her procedural questions was seemingly left with no other instructional option than to remove Patricia from the main part of the classroom.

In addition to speaking to the instructional context of the classroom, the event involving Patricia reveals the ideological perspective through which Connie saw literacy events, and hints at how this perspective might have influenced her classroom decision making. Because Patricia had recently come from a bilingual program, Connie believed she needed "extra help." This belief was consistent with Connie's view that her students' chief problem was that they relied too much on their Spanish. These beliefs were brought to the surface in the school's shift to English Only. Connie felt a renewed sense of optimism working in a school that had shifted away from bilingual education. She strongly identified with many of the tenets of Proposition 227. She connected those beliefs to her own familial experience and her thoughts about what it meant to be American:

It connects to my own personal experience in that the way my family and father was an immigrant and growing up and hearing all the stories about how my family came here and what they had to go through to get here. All the family separations, and all things that they had to put in place to make a life in this country. I get very upset when I hear about illegal immigrants coming in and getting government support when your family and the family you grew up in had to go through so much. I would not begrudge anybody for coming to America, I may sound a bit harsh, but I think we're just giving it too much and making it too easy. (Connie, Interview, PH #2)

Connie's ideological filter seemed to influence the way she saw Patricia. Connie believed that, in many ways, the school has "done too much" for the immigrant students (Interview, PH # 2). For Connie, the extreme example of doing too much was providing bilingual programs that she viewed as giving immigrants an unnecessary special privilege. In asides she made to me during the instructional day, Connie frequently sought to explain Patricia's behavior in terms of her "coming from a bilingual program." Connie often reported this fact to me after her one-on-one interactions with Patricia. Her insistence that Patricia needed more help based on her involvement in a bilingual program seemed to reveal Connie's deficit-based views about the students' use of Spanish. As an outside observer, I saw Patricia in a very different light. Patricia was an incredibly astute user of language—both in Spanish and English. She made jokes to her classmates in English in the small spaces of unofficial classroom talk, and once described Open Court blending to a classmate as "puro ruido" (pure noise).

An incident that happened towards the end of the year offered further evidence that the way Connie viewed classroom events was largely influenced by her ideological feelings regarding the language and culture of her students. After taking the end of the year Open Court comprehension assessment, Patricia scored at the top of the class. Connie did not consider that an ability to read in her first language may have helped Patricia, nor did Connie question whether she might have grouped Patricia inappropriately throughout the year. She did, however, lament that her high scores were probably going to keep her from qualifying to receive extra ESL help. Connie believed that was "a real shame" because, as a student who came from a bilingual program, she needed the extra help.

Reading: Who Talks and What They Talk About

> Collections for Young Scholars are organized so that each selection in a unit adds more information or a different perspective to the students' growing body of knowledge about a particular topic...As they explore increasingly complex and challenging unit concepts, students participate in writing, discussing, interviewing, debating, and other individual and collaborative activities that extend their experiences and offer opportunities for reflection. [This] provides English Language Learners opportunities to build on their existing knowledge and to use English to expand their understanding of a concept or a topic. (Second Grade Open Court Teachers Guide, 38F)

At the end of Phase 2 of my observations with Connie, I asked her about the reality of her and her students' experience of the story anthology compared with how the Open Court Experts viewed the event. She said, "That stayed pretty much the way they wanted it. The students' decoding is excellent. The fluency is getting better, but the speed just isn't there, but most of the students can handle the decoding now." Connie interpreted her main job in literacy instruction as ensuring the proper decoding skills for her students.

Her priority of ensuring the students developed proper decoding skills was evident throughout the observations of her reading practice. There were three main types of interactions between student and teacher in teacher run-reading events:

> Word Meaning. Connie asked the students about the meaning of an individual word. She used the word in a sentence until the students could supply a synonym.
> Conventions. Connie asked the students about the punctuation of a particular sentence, or she asked students to identify words that were particular parts of speech in the text.

Phonetic Exactness. Connie worked with the students to ensure the proper pronunciation of English words and phonemes.

Her emphasis on these three types of interactions was supported by the nature of the Step-by-Step books. The stories lacked strong plots and were primarily designed for "reading practice." During the reading of the books, Connie seldom asked questions regarding the story events or the plot. Connie often asked students to identify compound words or to circle long vowels. Such interaction contributed to the treatment of text as a puzzle. Texts were viewed as little more than the sum total of their phonetic or grammatical values.

Although the class did read "real stories" in the anthology, the patterns of interaction established in blending and the step-by-step books spilled over and shaped the nature of story reading events. In the following example, students were reading the story Fossils by Akali. The story was part of a unit in the Open Court Anthology about fossils that the class had just begun.

The class is sitting on the rug as Connie sits in a chair. They have just finished a brief discussion about a video on fossils. Michael, Salvador and Miguel were the only students who participated in the one-minute discussion.

After the discussion ends, Connie tells the students to open their books and says, "Today, I want us to read the story out loud. Tomorrow you can read it with your partner. I am expecting that we are all on the right page, and we are following along. I know you are going to get tired and bored because you know I get tired and bored listening. But, you know, we have to read it this way. OK, that is just one of the ways we have to do it."

Roberto is called on to read the first page of the story. He reads though without interruption from anyone and most of the class' 20 students follow along. Connie calls on Oscar to read next. He struggles a bit as he reads. When he mispronounces or misreads a word, Connie corrects him and provides the proper word or pronunciation. This pattern continues for four more students. Each student reads a page. Each student's misreadings are corrected by Connie.

Connie asks the class to read the next page out loud by themselves. Midway though their reading, she interrupts them and comments, "I am not hearing anybody on this side at all (She directs this to a group of four students who are at this point completely disengaged.).

Connie asks Michael to read. He reads confidently and loudly and finishes the page without interruption from Connie.

Table 6 Connie Classroom Excerpt: Reading Vocabulary		
Connie	*Students*	*Actions*
There is a whole bunch of vocabulary words on that page aren't there? What are some of the vocabulary words?		
	Michael: Seep	Michael calls out.
What did seep mean, who can tell me what seep means?		
	Michael: The water is falling.	
OK, it was going through the layers of mud, OK, sometimes when you have a leak maybe in your ceiling the water seeps through there and comes through. What is another vocabulary word?		
	Miguel: Mininals.	Miguel calls out after looking down at the book.

Table 6 Connie Classroom Excerpt: Reading Vocabulary		
Connie	*Students*	*Actions*
Minerals (With emphasis seemingly to correct his pronunciation). No minerals isn't one of our vocabulary words that you are doing for the test.

Scientist isn't on this page. I see one more on this page. (playfully angry) Some of you have already turned the page. Go back. Dissolve. What does dissolve mean? There are two more on this page that I see. | Oscar: Scientist. | |
| It's on the last line..

See that imprint on the mud there. OK, next page. | Salvador: (Calling out) Imprint. | |

Three more students take turns reading. The class has become increasingly fidgety with each turn of the page. As the third student is reading the last page of the story, many of the students are not following along. Macro plays with his shoes and a few of the girls seated in the corner opposite Connie begin to whisper to each other. Connie becomes quite frustrated with the students, passes out a story assessment, and sends the students to their desks to do the assessment individually.

This reading event was indicative of many of the realities of practice in this classroom. Obligation and boredom were the ways Connie framed this reading event for the children. The focus was not "how fossils are made." Student-teacher interaction was concerned only with phonetic correction and word meaning.

Teacher attention to word meaning was not permeable. In this case, the "test" determined which words were potential candidates for examination. Miguel's suggestion that "mininals" was one of the vocabulary words was not given any instructional attention by Connie. The nature of teacher and student interaction in this event reflects a literacy context that centered on the "basics" and seldom included meaning-based topics.

Connie's Individual Qualities and the Enactment of Practice

In addition to voting for Proposition 227, Connie was firmly convinced that changes brought about by Proposition 227 were going to really benefit her ELL students. Although she had been a bilingual teacher prior to the passage of Proposition 227, Connie was not a proficient speaker of Spanish. Connie had always "had a bilingual class," but the way the program had been set up, she never worked directly with her Latino students in primary language literacy development—that responsibility was relegated to bilingual teaching aides. While she had always been a teacher designated to teach in a bilingual program, she doesn't remember specifically requesting to be a bilingual teacher. At the time, she recalls, she didn't have a bilingual credential and "guesses that it (her teaching a bilingual class) was because" she was bilingual (Portuguese.) She said:

> I guess I don't know how I got assigned the bilingual class. I just have always taught the bilingual kids. I guess it was because I spoke because I was bilingual….but, in my family we knew it was really important to speak English. My father was always very critical of me being a bilingual teacher, and now I really feel like he was right. (Connie, Interview, PH #1)

These comments, considered with her feelings about her family's immigration history and her feelings about her Latino students, reveal her as a teacher whose own individual experience and ideology validated an English Only model. Connie invoked the same sort of argument that was made by many supporters of Proposition 227—"My grandma did, so why can't these kids?" Her views about language and the best way for kids to learn language directly influenced literacy instruction took in her class.

Connie's views about bilingual education and her personal history worked in dynamic relationship with her positioning as a teacher at Westway. For Connie, being a teacher at Westway had become dreadful. She expressed these feelings in relationship to her work within the Open Court Literacy series. She said, "Open Court is a dictatorship. As far as I am concerned this is a dictatorship. They dictate; we do. We're all just pawns doing exactly what they tell us to" (Connie, Interview, PH #1). Complicating this frustration was her belief that English Only and to a large extent the Open Court program were going to benefit her students greatly. While she deeply resented the grant, she was optimistic about the program itself. While she hated the pressure of Open Court monitoring, she felt confident that prohibiting her students from speaking Spanish in class would benefit them in the long run.

CONCLUSION: TEACHER POSITIONING AND LITERACY INSTRUCTION AT WESTWAY

Although Proposition 227 prescribed a uniform solution to the education of culturally and linguistically diverse students in California, the experiences and work of Celia and Connie in one school indicated that uniform solutions do not always achieve their intended results. Although the two teachers worked in a school with a highly controlled and regimented program of literacy instruction, the teachers negotiated the policy demands and the demands of the program in very different ways. While Celia's classroom was characterized by her attempt to facilitate full participation of her students through her use of Spanish and her cultural knowledge of her students, Connie's classroom context centered around her treatment of the language and culture of her students as a deficit and an emphasis on the "basics."

The contrast in Celia's and Connie's beliefs about their students, immigration, the value of primary language instruction, and their entry into the field of teaching highlights the roles that individual characteristics of teachers can play in the negotiation of literacy instruction. Celia saw her students' home language and culture as potential resources and struggled to find ways to utilize those resources in the new policy and instructional context created by English Only and Open Court. For Connie, English Only and Open Court were the perfect solution to fit the problem of immigrant students who came from home environments not conducive to school success. Two teachers in the same school, with the same program, yet the enactment of literacy instruction looked quite different in each of their rooms. In both cases, who the teachers were and the way they saw themselves and their immigrant students were deciding factors in the local enactment of policy.

CHAPTER 6

Literacy Practice at Open Valley

In this chapter, I address the connection between Angelica's and Elisa's experiences of the Proposition 227 decision-making process at their school and their enactment of literacy practice. I consider the classroom practice of each teacher in separate sections. In each section, I discuss the structure of literacy instruction and the nature of language use within that structure. I conclude each section with a discussion of the connection of the teacher's individual qualities and the local enactment of practice.

ANGELICA: A COMMITTED BILINGUAL EDUCATOR

> I need to stay here because if I don't do it who will?—I am not saying that nobody else is going to come and fight for the program, but I find it very hard for somebody new to come in and feel the way I feel and to see things that I see. Or, to have the desire within them that you have to have to go out there and fight. Because nobody is going to fight for your students but you. Nobody is going to go out there and try to get the support and help for the classroom that you want for your students. Nobody is going to do that. (Angelica, Interview, PH # 2)

Angelica frequently explained her role as a teacher at Open Valley in terms of fights, battles, and struggles. Such was the case during this interview. For a host of personal reasons, Angelica was considering taking a new teaching job at a school a few minutes from her home. Angelica lived 45 minutes from the school and had recently had her first child. The daily drive was beginning to take its toll. As she agonized about the possibility of leaving the school, Angelica highlighted one of the defining characteristics of her classroom practice: she created what she considered the best possible learning environment for her students situated in the larger national and state-wide debates surrounding the effectiveness and desirability of bilingual education.

Angelica often spoke of her work as a bilingual teacher as a direct response to forces in her own district and throughout the state that undermined bilingual education. She believed the action she took in her classroom was her way of "voting" (Interview, PH # 2) and participating in the decision-making process that affected her students. Although she described herself as "not a very political person" (Interview, PH # 1), she related her classroom literacy practice to larger social and political issues. These included Proposition 227 and the place of Open Valley's bilingual program in the district.

Her beliefs and self-defined role in the classroom were related to who she was as a teacher and the types of experiences she had in her own education. In addition, her response to the new policy context was influenced by her feelings and perceptions of the district's and school's response to Proposition 227. For Angelica, literacy instruction was one of the key times in the instructional day that she felt she could address the academic and social needs of her students. Her perceptions of these needs and her enactment of practice were largely influenced by her relations *to* and experience *of* the Proposition 227 decision-making structures at the school and district level.

In this section of the chapter, I will examine how Angelica's ideological response to Proposition 227 and her individual qualities influenced the nature of enacted literacy practice in her classroom. I will examine Angelica's use of reading groups to illustrate the connection between policy and practice. I will describe the structure and purpose of literacy events as they related to Angelica's enactment of practice. I will then consider how the structure of literacy instruction was related to Angelica's positioning vis-à-vis Proposition 227 implementation decisions.

Angelica's Classroom. Angelica's second-grade primary language classroom contained between 15 and 20 students. Because the school served a number of migrant students, these numbers varied throughout the year. The class consisted of approximately 75% male students. Nearly all of the students lived in the small community of Open Valley, which was a behind the school, and most of the parents of the students worked in the agricultural fields surrounding the school. All students wore the obligatory school uniform, consisting of blue pants and white shirts for boys and blue dresses and white shirts for girls.

Nearly all of Angelica's students were born in Mexico or Central America. The community in which they lived was composed primarily of recent immigrants. Consequently, students spoke Spanish almost exclusively in academic and social settings. A handful of students seemed to have more exposure to English and were more active participants in ELD activities. During ELD interaction, Angelica only spoke in English. While Angelica encouraged the students not to speak Spanish, she did accept answers in Spanish.

During all other instructional events, Angelica used Spanish. In the rare cases that students spoke English during Spanish literacy events, Angelica encouraged and praised their use of English.

Spanish was the language of literacy instruction. Literacy instruction began at 9:30 and ended before the students went to lunch at 11:15. Before the language arts block began, Angelica and the students participated in "tribes," which was a sharing opportunity for the students. Each day, Angelica posed a question to the class dealing with some aspect of their personal or academic lives, and students had a turn to share their feelings or thoughts about the topic. After Tribes, Angelica explained and assigned independent seat work the students did while she worked with reading groups. Generally, seat work was listed on the overhead under the heading, "Hoy tu responsibilidad es" [Today your responsibility is]. The independent seat work ranged from skill practice and silent reading to journal writing and various other activities associated with Cuentomundos, the language arts series used in the room.

As students began seat work, Angelica had 30-second conferences with each student. During the conferences, Angelica reviewed homework with the students as well as checking in on academic and personal matters.

The centerpiece of her literacy instruction was reading groups. Three ability groups all read the same material using the Cuentomundo series. Angelica considered moving reading instruction to the whole group, but felt the smaller groups allowed her more flexibility in working with students. Angelica generally spent one week on each story. After recess at 1:15, Angelica conducted ELD time using the series Into English.

During classroom instruction, Angelica maintained a very business-like and serious demeanor with her students. Angelica was an efficient and skilled classroom manger, and it was rare that she had to give directions to a single student or the whole class more than once.

Students sat in four rows of five desks facing the front of the room. During reading instruction, students moved to the back of the room and sat with Angelica at a small kidney-shaped reading table. Students spent time on the rug during sharing time and story reading.

ANGELICA: LITERACY HER OWN WAY

To understand the structure of literacy events and the role that language played in those events, I will examine teacher and student interaction during reading group instruction. The reading group events illustrated Angelica's instructional priorities and her attempts to address those priorities. By examining classroom literacy events against Angelica's individual characteristics and her experiences with Proposition 227 implementation, I hope to explore the connection between policy and practice and highlight the role Angelica played in the enactment of policy.

Reading Groups

> I don't want them to only read and decode, but I want them to comprehend. My goal. Yea, I taught the student how to read, but I just don't want decoders, and my reading groups and the questions I use in the reading groups have helped me do that. (Angelica, Interview, PH # 2)

Angelica's focus on comprehension permeated a great deal of her literacy instruction. It played a large role in her decision to use ability groups during reading. While she frequently considered moving to mixed ability groups or whole class instruction for reading, she felt small group instruction offered the best chance to allow students time to talk to her and each other. Angelica believed that such conversation would allow students to "see themselves in the story," a process she believed was directly connected to their reading comprehension.

Although she used the teacher's guide as a source of instructional activities during the small group reading, she put a great deal of herself in the interaction with the students. Describing the role the curriculum guide played in her literacy group instruction, she said:

> I take and choose what I think is going to benefit my kids. So, I don't just say: I am not going to do this because I don't like it, but I try to pick activities to increase their comprehension, their decoding, and make them critical thinkers. I am not just going to choose any old activity. (Angelica, Interview, PH # 1)

In each activity and interaction with her students, Angelica seemed to address her goals for her students directly. Literacy events provided multidimensional participatory structures for children to "put themselves in the story." Angelica's language use during such interaction created instructional space to draw upon students' existing cultural and academic knowledge in the negotiations of written texts. Interactions between Angelica and her students centered around the following types:

> Conventions. Angelica asked students about the functions of particular aspects of the Spanish language. These types of interactions were generally related to an element of a story the class was reading.
> Phonetic Exactness. Comments that drew focus to the decoding of individual sounds of words. These comprised a small part of classroom interactions and were generally related to an element of a story the class was reading.
> Events of Story Question. Questions soliciting retelling or summaries of events from a story.
> Creating/building on Intertextuality. Comments or questions that drew upon the students' social and cultural

lives as resources in understanding the stories the class
read.

Concept Question. Questions that asked students to draw
conclusions or make inferences about an event in a story.

Turn Extension. Comment or question by Angelica that
facilitated students' turns at talk. A unique feature of
these interactions was that they often occurred after the
students had responded incorrectly to one of Angelica's
questions.

While Conventions and Phonetic Exactness were part of Angelica's
interaction with the students, they occurred less often than they did in
the classrooms at Westway. Interactions that centered on Building on
Intertextuality and Turn Extensions were very prominent features of
Angelica's classroom.

Multidimensional Student Participation

In coding the field notes from Angelica's classroom, I identified several
instances where teacher-student interaction had multidimensional
structure. That is, all conversation did not begin and end with the
teacher. Angelica's questions often elicited a wave of answers from
students that contributed to a collective understanding about a
particular story or concept the children were discussing. The
interactional structure of the reading group events seemed to mirror
Angelica's desire to have the children see themselves in the story.
These patterns of interaction were evident as Angelica's top group
worked on pre-reading activities for the story "Enrique and Pancho."

The students in Angelica's top group sit at the small reading
table in the back corner of the room. Clockwise from Angelica
sit Maria, Roberto, Miguel, Rosa, Ernesto, Sandra, Xochi. The
reading group activity begins with a review of the vocabulary
words from the story. Angelica asks the group to preview the
story. At Angelica's request, the group turns through the pages
of the story which, chronicles an only child's attempt to
convince his parents to buy him a dog. The dog, Pancho,
serves as a protective force in Enrique's life. After the parents
buy him the dog, he has a new, confident view of himself.
Previewing the story consists of rapid exchanges, with

Angelica asking the students what they think will happen at "this point" or "that point" of the story. Angelica regulates students' turns by looking in the direction of the student who was speaking, or calling directly on students to take a turn.

Angelica asks the students to turn to page 70, which has a picture of Pancho as a puppy. Page 71 is full of dog collars of all different colors and sizes.

Table 7 Angelica Classroom Excerpt: Collars Discussion		
Angelica	*Students*	*Action*
OK, ¿Qué miran en la página setenta?		
	Rosa: Un Perrito	Miguel's response
	Miguel: Un perro	follows immediately
¿Está grande o	chiqu**ito**.	after Rosa's. Miguel
chiquito?		has a pleased looked
	Ss: Chiquito.	on his face when he
	Roberto: Lo van	rhymes his last word
	[The parents] a	with Rosa's.
¿Que miran en la	comprar.	
página sesenta y		
uno?	Ss: (Excitedly)	
	Collares.	
¿Por qué hay tantos		
collares de		
diferentes tamaños?	[At this point several	
	students overlap	
	each other. Their	Angelica gives the
	answers, although	students a few
	slightly different,	moments to call out
	center around	their answers. Most
	"Porque el niño	of them do call out
	tiene que escoger el	an answer. They
	mejor para el	seem to speaking to
(Raising her voice	perro."]	each other as much
slightly) ¿Quién más		as they directly
puede opinar? Ha		address their
pasado mucho		teacher.

Table 7 Angelica Classroom Excerpt: Collars Discussion

Angelica	Students	Action
tiempo desde que oíamos de Xochi.	Xochi: Este Pancho seria diferentes tamaños, entonces los collares tienen que ser de diferentes tamaños también.	As Xochi, who has a very quiet voice, speaks, the class falls silent.
Cambien la página, (In a dry tone) Quién está allí?		The students turn to page 72.
	Ss: (Flatly) Un perro. Roberto: Oh, (enthusiastically) Pancho! Miguel: (waving his arms to be called on)	Roberto points to the picture of the grown dog.
(playfully) Entonces, por qué nos enseñaron tantos collares en la página 71?	Creció.	
	Ss: (very animated) Creció. Carolina: Iba a crecer y y Migulel: (Looking at Carolina and picking her at her second "y") Oh, Oh, porque creció más grande y necesitaba nuevos collares.	Angelica asks the group to look back to page 70 and compare the puppy on that page with the dog on 72.

Table 8 English Translation of Collars Discussion		
Angelica	*Students*	*Action*
OK, what do you see on page 70?		
	Rosa: A dog	Miguel's response
	Miguel: A small dog	follows immediately
Is it big or small?		after Rosa's. Miguel
	Ss: Small	has a pleased looked
	Roberto: The	on his face when he
	parents are going to	rhymes his last word
	buy it.	with Rosa's.
What do you see on page 71?		
	Ss: (Excitedly) Dog collars.	
Why are there so many collars of different sizes?		
	[At this point several students overlap each other. Their answers, although slightly different, center around "Because the kid has to pick the best one for the dog."]	Angelica gives the students a few moments to call out their answers. Most of them do call out an answer. They seem to speaking to each other as much as they directly address their teacher.
(Raising her voice slightly) Who else can give us an opinion? A long time has passed since we heard from Xochi.		
	Xochi: The dog is going to be different sizes, so the collars have to be different sizes, too.	As Xochi, who has a very quite voice, speaks the class falls silent.
Turn the page, (In a dry tone) Who is on it?		The students turn to page 72.

Table 8 English Translation of Collars Discussion		
Angelica	*Students*	*Action*
	Ss: (Flatly) A dog. Roberto: Oh, (enthusiastically) Pancho! Miguel: (waving his arms to be called on) He grew up!	Roberto points to the picture of the grown dog.
(playfully) So, then why did they show us so many collars on page 71.	Ss: (very animated) He grew up.	Angelica asks the group to look back to page 70 and compare the puppy on that page with the dog on 72.
	Carolina: He was going to grow and and Miguel: (Looking at Carolina and picking her at her second "and") Oh, because he grew bigger and needed the collars.	

In this exchange with the students, Angelica's focus on comprehension manifested itself in the manner in which she previewed the story. During story previewing in reading group events, Angelica invited students to share their experiences in relation to the story. This invitation positioned students as active participants in instructional conversations.

In this exchange, the multidimensional participant structure that characterized many of the literacy interactions in the room was evident. When Angelica asked, "What was on page 72?," she elicited three responses from her students. Her turn regulation of student talk struck a balance between control and flexibility. This balance created an environment in which students could participate in a natural way without talking over one another. A single question from Angelica lead the three students to build on each other's responses and collectively conclude that the big dog on page 72 was the puppy who appeared on page 70.

The group's discussion regarding the numerous collars was indicative of the role of that student input in determining the meaning of written texts. As students discussed how the collars might fit into the plot of the story, they generated ideas that guided them through their reading of the text. The ideas that were generated were closely connected to the open and flexible nature of the questions that Angelica asked. Although Angelica posed questions regarding the collars in the opening of the lesson, she only re-visited the issue after Miguel came to the conclusion that the dog on page 72 was the grown puppy from page 70. Although the student's answers to Angelica's initial question regarding the collars were slightly off the mark, Angelica waited until the students had discovered the answers on their own before stressing the picture's connection to the overall meaning of the story. The structure of this literacy event allowed students to actively participate in meaning-making activities. Over the course of days that followed this event, students maintained the same level of enthusiasm and engagement as they read. Their engagement in the previewing event created moment for a successful learning context.

In addition to the multidimensional nature of student participation in reading group events, this exchange between Angelica and her students highlights how "wrong answers" were treated in literacy discussions. Although the students' responses to Angelica's question about the collars were slightly off the mark, Angelica did not directly correct the students or attempt to guide them immediately to a response that more accurately reflected the meaning of the story. Instead, Angelica treated student "wrong answers" as opportunities for learning. She seldom corrected student responses in a "you're wrong" fashion. Often, as in this case, Angelica left the wrong answers "on the table," and attempted to guide students back to a point where they could re-examine their initial responses.

Putting the Students in the Story

Angelica believed that students' reading comprehension would improve if students were able to "see themselves in the story." She felt this was particularly true of her low reading group. Her work with many of the students in the low group reflected her self-described role as a fighter for her students. She made frequent visits to their homes, had daily communication with their parents, recorded the weekly story on audio tapes for the students to take home, and had many informal help sessions after school with them. She viewed all such actions as part of the "struggle" that was necessary for students to achieve in her classroom.

In her perpetual "fight" for her students, Angelica learned a great deal about the lives of her students. She learned about their families, their siblings, and their home environments. Her knowledge of the students' social worlds frequently came up in her interactions with them. Angelica often used the knowledge she had to help her students negotiate the stories they read. In helping the students access this knowledge, she used a questioning strategy that facilitated student participation. This strategy was evident as she worked with her low reading group on the second day of the group's work with the Enrique and Pancho story. On the first day, she had given the students extended turns to talk about their experience with pets in their homes and neighborhoods. Over the course of reading the story, Angelica frequently drew upon those discussions in her questions about the story.

During this event, Angelica integrated knowledge about her student directly into the instructional discourse:

> The six boys of Angelica's A group are seated at the reading table—it is a group consisting of Angelica's lowest students whom she claims will all be reading above grade level at the end of the year. The boys are about to read the story "Enrique y Pancho."

> On the white board that is directly behind the reading table is a pre-reading graphic that relates to the story.

En una familia pequeña	En una familia grande
Juegas solo	

> Angelica tells the students they are going to read a story about a narrator who is an only child, and that she wants them to think about what life might be like for an only child. As

Angelica begins to ask her initial questions, she stands up and motions at the graphic organizer on the white board.

Table 9 Angelica Classroom Excerpt: "In a Small Family"		
Angelica	*Students*	*Actions*
En un a familia pequeña juegas solo, ¿que tienes que hacer en una familia grande? Cesar. (Sternly) Piensa. Si en una familia pequeña juegas solo-- que tú nada más fueras el único niño en tu casa-- Tú tienes que jugar con tus juguetes solito, ¿verdad? Y si está Anna (his sister) y todos tus hermanitos, ¿qué debes hacer con tus juguetes? ¿Qué se debe hacer con tus juguetes si están todos tus hermanitos en tu casa? ¿Tú juegas con quién?	Cesar: Eh, (quickly and chewing his words) Yo no sé. Cesar: (looking up with a sort of "you caught me grin") ¿Si alguien estaba? Cesar: ¿Eh? Cesar: Juegan. Cesar: Con mi hermano.	As Angelica is asking the question, Cesar has pushed his chair three feet away from the reading table. He is looking around the room with a blank stare. Juan who raised his hand after Angelica's initial questions has a strained look on his face--as if he can't wait to participate. His hand was initially raised, but he lowers it as Angelica talks to Cesar. His facial expression never diminishes.

Table 9 Angelica Classroom Excerpt: "In a Small Family"

Angelica	Students	Actions
¿No más con él o con todos? A ver, dime en una oración.	Cesar: Con todos… (Continuing off of his last comment) …Ya no, mi hermano y Anna no pueden jugar juntos, y este	
OK, pero Cesar. Si tú juegas solo en tu casa, y como tú tienes una familia grande, qué debes hacer. ¿Compartir o jugar solo?	Cesar: Compartir con otros. (pauses and smiles) Tengo que compartir mis juguetes.	
Muy bien, ¿están de acuerdo con Cesar? Voy a poner juegues con otros.	Other boys: (With enthusiasm) Sí! Juan: (speaking out without being formally acknowledged by Angelica) Iba a decir compar compar Juan: (Excitedly to the rest of the group). Es lo que iba a decir. Juego con todos.	Angelica writes "Juegues con los otros" in the column under "Una famila grande."

Table 10 English Translation of "In a Small Family"		
Angelica	*Student*	*Action*
In a small family you play alone, what do you have to do in a big family? Cesar.		As Angelica is asking the question, Cesar has pushed his chair three feet away from the reading table. He is looking around the room with a blank stare.
	Cesar: Eh, (quickly and chewing his words) I don't know.	
(Sternly) Think, if in a small family you play alone—and you are the only kid in your house—You have to play alone, right?		
	Cesar: (looking up with a sort of "you caught me grin") If someone is there?	
And if Anna is there and all your brother and sisters, what do you have to do with your toys?		Juan who raised his hand after Angelica's initial questions has a strained look on his face--as if he can't wait to participate. His hand was initially raised, but he lowers it as Angelica talks to Cesar. His facial expression never diminishes.
	Cesar: Eh?	
What do you have to do with your toys if all your brothers and sisters are in the house?		
	Cesar: They play.	
Who do you play with?		
	Cesar: With my brother.	
Only with him or with the others?		
	Cesar: With the others…	
OK, give me a sentence.		
	(Continuing off of	

Table 10 English Translation of "In a Small Family"		
Angelica	*Student*	*Action*
	his last comment) …Now no, my brother and Anna can't play together because…	
OK, but Cesar. If you play alone in the house, and how you have a large family, what do you have to do? Share or play alone?		
	Cesar: Share with the others. (pauses and smiles) I have to share my toys.	
Very good. Do you agree with Cesar?		
	Other boys: Yes!	
I am going to write plays with others.	Juan: (speaking out without being formally acknowledge by Angelica) I was going to say sha shar. That is what I was going to say. I play with everyone.	
		A writes "You play with the others" in the column under "A large family."

This exchange and the questioning strategy used by Angelica demonstrated the role students' home culture had in shaping the nature of literacy instruction. By capitalizing on her knowledge of Cesar's home life, Angelica gave him a way to be a meaningful participant in this discussion that he had otherwise started to tune out of. The knowledge she had of his family had come from the many visits she had made to his home. Her knowledge of his social world served as an instructional life preserver allowing Cesar to construct a response to a question that he was struggling to respond to.

Similarly, the nature of the discussion and the shape it took had the effect of keeping all students engaged—even Juan—who, although he was not able to participate in the direct exchange, was still able to share, "That this is what I was going to say." Angelica set the stage for this exchange by informing the boys that they were having this discussion for a particular reason—a reason directly connected to their ability to relate to the story they were about to read. Her ability to draw on this information was a major influence in determining the context of literacy in this room.

Summary of Classroom Practice: A Culture of Meaning

Angelica's focus on comprehension had many manifestations in the classroom. Angelica's willingness to allow students space to explore the meaning of stories and her ability to connect those explorations with their lives were defining elements of the overall context of the classroom. The examples of reading group interaction indicated that Angelica structured literacy instruction to allow multidimensional participation. Additionally, Angelica structured events in a way that allowed students' wrong answers to be used as a point of departure for further exploration and discussion.

Angelica used many types of instructional structures and arrangements, but the reading group set the stage for the kind of interaction that transcended most story reading and group reading events. Literacy instruction in other areas, including read-a-louds and writing, followed the pattern evident in the literacy events presented in this section. Angelica clearly articulated the purpose for each activity, and students were invited to be active participants in experiencing the defined purpose. Angelica's questions in literacy events focused on expanding student participation, and students were always eager participants. Angelica's focus on meaning and her instructional strategies worked to create a culture of meaning in the classroom. When interaction focused on "Phonetic Exactness" and "Conventions," it occurred as the students were pursuing the meaning of the stories they read. As the students read with Angelica or with each other, they frequently evoked the meaning-based reading strategies Angelica stressed in her own teaching. The questions "se vea bien, se suena bien, y tiene sentido" (does it look good, does it sound good, does it make sense) were frequently used by students to help each other read through the materials Angelica used in classroom literacy events.

Angelica's Individual Characteristics and the Enactment of Literacy Instruction

Angelica conceived of her chief purpose in literacy instruction as making sure the children became critical thinkers and could "put themselves in the stories" they read. These priorities manifested themselves in the instructional decisions Angelica made during literacy instruction. Angelica made conscious choices to facilitate student participation, and she drew upon students' home and cultural resources in the negotiations of written texts. These strategies employed in her room created a very "un-227" context for instruction.

Angelica's purposes and actions in literacy instruction were reflected in who she was as a teacher—particularly her entry into the field of teaching and her deep commitment to bilingual education. Angelica's attempts to make sure that the pedagogy of her room fit the cultural and academic needs of her students was a direct response to her own educational history. Angelica described her education in terms of exclusion, suffering, and isolation. She drew upon these memories to describe why she became a bilingual teacher. She detailed how, in the fall of 1998 following the passage of Proposition 227, she helped make the case to parents to sign the waiver to maintain the school's bilingual program. The meeting was quite a contentious affair with one parent attempting to convince the other parents not to sign the waiver. Angelica recalled the meeting in the following way:

> ...I even used myself as an example. It's very embarrassing, but I told the parents this story to show them why I believe in

bilingual education. I believe in bilingual education because I was forced to be in schools and I was forced to be with teachers that weren't bilingual. Because my parents didn't have a choice because we used to live in LA. I told them (the parents at the meeting) I was a first grader and the teacher passed out these small white paper plates, I still remember this, and she put this white stuff in it. I mean se miraba igual que el arroz que hacia mi mama (It looked exactly like the rice that my mom made.) But, it was paste. The teacher said "we are going to give you paste." Yea, she said it. But, I didn't understand. And do you know what I did with that paste, parents [meaning the parents at the waiver meeting]? I ate it. The teacher sent me to get tested for special Ed. because I ate paste. (Her she raises her voice recapturing the contentious exchange with the parent who did not want her child to be in bilingual education). Now, do you think I was a child who needed a special day class or a child who had something wrong with its mind. No, it was because I didn't know what the teachers said. And I told the parents at the meeting, I am not going to tell you about the many other things that happened to me because it is just too sad. But let me tell you if you want your children to suffer then put them in an English-Only school. And by doing that you are a sending your children the message—I taught you how to talk in Spanish, but I really don't want you to, I really don't care. (Angelica, Interview, PH # 1)

Angelica's comments are powerful reminders that the individual characteristics of teachers play a significant role in the local enactment of policy. Long before Proposition 227 had the chance to take effect in her classroom, Angelica was shaping the nature of the effect through her work in securing the parental waivers. Her entry into the field was directly related to an embarrassing moment around her home culture and language. Her classroom in many ways seemed to be a response to that embarrassing moment through the many instances that she used the home culture of the students as an instructional resource. Through her use of questioning strategies, she created a classroom where literacy instruction made space for the home culture and language of her students.

Angelica's entry into the field and her own educational experiences were two individual characteristics that influenced the local enactment of policy in her classroom. These two factors functioned as guiding forces in the creation of her classroom practice.

Angelica's deep ideological commitment to bilingual education also played a significant role in the local enactment of her literacy practice. For Angelica, the manner in which she constructed her literacy practice made good sense culturally, socially, and academically. She saw her role in the classroom as meeting the desire of the parents at Open Valley. Her perception of those needs and her commitment to fulfill them were major factors in her negotiation of literacy instruction at the school. In response to an interview question regarding the claim of Proposition 227 that immigrant parents wanted their children to learn English, Angelica said:

> I think he's [Unz] thinking for some of them. He's talking about a very, very small group of people. These immigrants that he's talking about are people that have completely assimilated into this culture. Let's talk about the Open Valley parents here. These parents here do not believe this. Our parents are very concerned about their children losing their language. They don't want to lose their culture and that's why they believe the same philosophy and they have our [the teachers'] philosophy…Yes it is hard to remain a bilingual. But, if you don't give them basis—the foundation that the child needs to use against the second language—it's not going to happen. Basically, we are all here in this America. And, we do all need to speak the language of this country, but that doesn't mean that we have to let go of our language. (Angelica, Interview, PH # 2)

Angelica's belief that learning English and learning Spanish were not competing goals was at the heart of her local enactment of practice. She designed her classroom to ensure the first-language literacy needs of her students were met and she worried about little else. Her close communication with the parents of her students and her interpretation of their goals seemed to be the only compass she needed to navigate the new policy context created by Proposition 227.

ELISA: LOOKING FOR GUIDANCE IN INSTRUCTION

I didn't know exactly what they needed for English reading. I don't know if they need practice with the sounds or can just take advantage of being fluent readers in Spanish. *Nadie me dijo* [nobody told me], "Elisa, do this test and it's going to tell you if the kids need to know the sounds. Do this paper, or by talking to the kids it's going to tell you if they know the sounds. Nobody really gave me anything. (Elisa, Interview, PH #2)

As the third-grade teacher in Open Valley's bilingual program, Elisa was responsible for transitioning the students from Spanish to English. For Elisa, the complexity of this task was compounded by her experience of the new policy context created by the school's Proposition 227 implementation decisions. The curricular freedom created by the Charter status did little to allay Elisa's confusion surrounding transition issues for her students. The nature of literacy instruction in Elisa's room was influenced by her insecurities about the students' development of English and her perception that the school offered her little help in resolving those insecurities.

During Phase 1 of the research, Elisa was concerned that the school had not yet "picked a transition program" and had yet to decided on a textbook series to use for the program. The third-grade students were supposed to receive one-half year of instruction in their primary language and some ELD instruction. By the second half of the year, instruction was to shift to second language development. Although she was well aware of the demands of the school's program, Elisa felt quite confused about how to meet those demands. She expressed these sentiments to Helen, the school's principal:

Y al principio del año tambien le dije a Helen. Fui a su oficina y le dije, sabe que siento confundida, y no se realmente que esperan de mi, que saque de ese programa.

[And at the beginning of the year, I went to Helen. I went to her office and I told her, do you know what I feel very confused about your expectations of me. I feel very confused

about what you want from this program.] (Elisa, Interview, PH
2)

Elisa believed that members of the school community were too
interested in maintaining the outward appearance that everything was
working well to take a serious look at the needs of the transition
program.

Counter-balancing the confusion Elisa felt about transition issues
were her instructional priorities. Elisa was a dedicated teacher who
developed an after-school academic help program for the school's
primary grade students. In part based on her own childhood experience
as a migrant farm-worker, she held a deep commitment to helping her
students become critical thinkers. It was in the space between the
confusion that she felt about her task and her commitment to seeing her
students through the process that literacy instruction took shape in her
classroom.

In this section, I will focus primarily on data collected from two
periods during Phase #2 of the research to examine how Elisa
negotiated the demands of English literacy instruction. I will first focus
on:

How was English Literacy instruction structured in the
classroom?
How did Elisa use Spanish and English in these literacy
events?

After describing the nature of practice in the room, I will consider how
her negotiation of literacy practice was related to her individual
qualities and characteristics.

Elisa's Classroom. Elisa's classroom was characterized by
constant change—both in the numbers of students and her instructional
arrangement of those students. The number of students in Elisa's room
at any time ranged from 11 to 20. The variation was due in large part to
the number of students whose parents were migrant farm-workers. In
addition, during Spanish and English literacy instruction, there was a
great deal of intra-class movement. Elisa received and sent students to
two other classrooms in the school. The number of students that
entered or left her classroom varied greatly over the year. All of the

students who traveled in and out of the Elisa's third grade classroom spoke Spanish as a first language.

Spanish was the language of choice for the students in and out of classroom settings. On the playground, students spoke almost exclusively in Spanish. During Phase 1 of the research in which literacy instruction focused on primary language development, Elisa and the students spoke almost exclusively in Spanish. During Phase 2 when the focus on instruction became English, Elisa's language use was a flexible combination of both Spanish and English. During English instructional events students were eager and willing to speak English.

The schedule and events of instruction in Elisa's room were in a constant state of evolution and flux. During Phase 1, primary language literacy instruction was scheduled between 9:00 and 10:30. Students participated in a variety of activities including reading stories and doing activity sheets from the language arts series Cuentomundos, reading short novels and writing journal entries associated with those novels, completing skill-based activities such as vocabulary practice, and practicing grammar rules. English Language Development using the Hampton Brown ESL program was scheduled for the afternoon. Elisa was not entirely enthusiastic about the Hampton Brown series because she felt it was not comprehensive enough to address the English needs of her students, and consequently it was often skipped.

During Phase 2 of my observations, instruction shifted dramatically. The transition program Elisa designed was centered around "guided reading." The make up of the groups and the activities done in the groups seemed to change daily. Some days the groups read English trade books, and other days they read poems. While students were not working with Elisa or the student teacher in a guided reading group, they worked in centers. The nature of assigned tasks during centers also shifted and evolved. The centers were developed in early March.

Students were given a great deal of latitude and free movement in the class. One of Elisa's main instructional goals was for the children to "talk to and learn from each other." The arrangements of the students represented this priority. During literacy instruction, students sat at small circular tables. The students worked in mixed-ability groups of their own choosing. The group sizes ranged between three and five students.

The Nature of Literacy Instruction

In order to describe the structure of literacy events in Elisa's classroom, I will focus on the English "guided reading" events for several methodological reasons. First, programmatically Elisa was defined as the "transition teacher." Her struggles to define and fulfill this role constituted one of the defining factors of her work at the school. Because my aim is to understand the new policy context created by Proposition 227 through the eyes of teachers, Elisa's identification of "transition" as her most important and difficult issue was central in my decision to select it as a point of analysis. Second, I am interested in teachers' negotiations of literacy practice. No element of Elisa's classroom literacy instruction represents negotiation more than her development and implementation of the transition program. The transition program Elisa developed was the result of months of struggle and agony with Hampton Brown's Into English and Open Court's Transition Review Program.

In January, Helen, the school's principal, directed Elisa to use a component of the Open Court as part of her transition program. The component, "Transition Review," was a supplement to the Open Court Curriculum that reinforced skills learned in the program. In the regular administration of the Open Court program, "Transition Review" was used as a transition between the 1st and 2nd grade curriculum. Like the use of the Open Court program at Westway, during the brief manifestation of Open Court in Elisa's third-grade class, the students worked on English language development by practicing sound spelling cards, blending, and reading predicable texts and poems. Once again, the Open Court emphasis was on "the sounds."

From the beginning, Elisa felt her students needed more than Transition Review. Having only these supplemental materials, Elisa was not entirely aware of the structure of the Open Court program. For their parts, the students seemed bored and uninterested in the program. The general buzz and engaged conversation that had characterized my observations during Phase 1 were gone. The Transition Review was first conducted in the large group, and then was gradually incorporated into the guided reading program Elisa was developing.

Guided Reading: A Mixed Context

After months of struggling with what to do, Elisa decided she would use guided reading small groups during her students' transition. She had received training from one of the school's reading specialists on guided reading and thought it could be an answer to some of her transition problems. Elisa had a student teacher working in her room during the second semester. For Elisa, the student teacher's presence was an extra motivation to work in small groups because while she worked with a group, the student teacher could circulate amongst the other students to answer questions and monitor their work.

My observations of Elisa's classroom during Phase 2 indicated that her use of guided reading was continually evolving. The grouping of students changed daily during the first weeks of March, but had stabilized by late April. The nature of work students did at the centers shifted, as did the kind of tasks the students were given in guided reading groups. Each day brought new changes. Elisa attributed some of the changes to the fact that she was designing the transition program on her own with minimal guidance from other members of the school community.

The instructional practice in the room reflected many tensions present during the design of the transition program. Classroom practice also revealed Elisa's views about language and her convictions about how and in what environment her immigrant students should be educated. Interactions between Elisa and her students centered around the following types:

> Word Meaning. Elisa offered or solicited Spanish
> translations of words in stories.
> Phonetic Exactness. Teacher comments focused on the
> sounds of individual letters or decoding words. This
> became a prominent feature when Elisa used materials
> from the Open Court program.
> Events of Story Question. Questions soliciting retelling or
> summary of events from a story.
> Creating/building on Intertextuality. Comments or
> questions that drew upon students' social and cultural
> lives as resources in understanding stories the class read.

Concept Question. Questions that asked students to draw
conclusions or make inferences about events or concepts
in stories. During English instruction, Elisa encouraged
students to respond in Spanish if they were not able to do
so in English.
Turn Extension. Comments or questions by Elisa that
extended student turns.

In this section, I will consider three guided reading events in an attempt
to illuminate the structure of literacy instruction in the room and the
role that Spanish played in instruction. In the concluding section, I will
consider how the local enactment of policy in Elisa's room was related
to her positioning at the school and her individual qualities.

*The First Day of English Guiding Reading: "Porque Lo Hicimos
en Español?"* On the first day of English guided reading, Elisa lead
each of the groups through a series of activities in Spanish. Each of the
five groups examined a picture of an animal. Elisa solicited comments
from the students about the animal. After a conversation about the
picture, Elisa gave the students five minutes to write a few sentences
about the picture. The following conversation happened between Elisa
and the second group, which included Ernesto, Rosa, Cristóbal, Betty,
and Daniel after they had concluded the activity.

Table 11 Classroom Excerpt Elisa: First day of English Reading		
Elisa	*Students*	*Action*
OK, ayúdame. Qué es lo que estamos haciendo? Por qué estamos haciendo esto?	Ernesto: (dutifully) Aprender. Rosa: Para aprender los dibujos. Cristóbal: Para aprender más palabras.	All the students have raised their hands and she is calling on them by touching her hand in front of the students.

Table 11 Classroom Excerpt Elisa: First day of English Reading		
Elisa	*Students*	*Action*
Para aprender palabras?	Rosa: Para hacer como agarrar palabras de un dibujo.	
[Elisa repeats Rosa's response.] Y para... lo que dijiste ahorita. Si ven como hacerlo en español.	Cristóbal: (takes turn without hand up) Para aprender el inglés.	
Y cómo vamos aprender el inglés.		
	Ernesto: Aprendiendo palabras.	
Aprendiendo palabras.		
	Elsa: (Hand up-- Officially recognized) Tenemos que saber como lo hacemos en español primero y luego es más fácil hacerlo en inglés.	At this point the pace of the discussion quickens.
Si cuando estamos con un dibujo, y tenemos palabras, y de las palabras qué hacemos?		
De estas oraciones qué podemos hacer?	Daniel: Oraciones!	
De un párrafo qué podemos hacer?	Ss: Párrafo.	
	Ss: Un capítulo	

Table 11 Classroom Excerpt Elisa: First day of English Reading		
Elisa	*Students*	*Action*
	Un resumen Ensayos.	
Qué tiene que ver esto con el inglés?		
	Daniel: Yo voy a saber las palabras que tiene que responder.	
	Betty: Puedes poner *tree* en vez de árbol (She is pointing at the white board where Elisa had written some of the sentences students generated.)	
Si saben las palabras en inglés, podemos hacer oraciones en inglés.		
	Ss: Sí.	
Y luego podemos hacer párrafos.		
	Ss: Sí.	
Luego podemos hacer ensayos en inglés.		After Betty's comments Elisa asks the students "what can I put in place of..." with each of the Spanish words they had used to describe the picture. The students excitedly call out the English words.

Table 12 English Translation of First Day of English Reading		
Elisa	*Students*	*Action*
Ok, help me out. What are we doing? Why are we doing this?	Ernesto: (dutifully) To learn. Rosa: To learn about drawings. Cristóbal: To learn words.	All the students have raised their hands and she is calling on them by touching her hand in front of the students.
To learn words?	Rosa: To learn how to take words from a picture.	
[E repeats Rosa's response.] And for... What did you just say? You can see how we do it in Spanish. And, how are we going to learn English?	Cristóbal: To learn English.	
Learning words.	Ernesto: Learning words.	
	Elsa: (Hand up-- Officially recognized) We have to know how to do it in Spanish first and then it will easier to do it in English.	
Yes, and when we are working with a picture, and we have words, from the words what do we		At this point the pace of the discussion quickens.

Elisa	Students	Action
Table 12 English Translation of First Day of English Reading		
make?	Daniel: Sentences	
And from those sentences what can you do?		
	Ss: Paragraphs.	
From one paragraph what can we do?		
	Ss: A chapter A summary An essay	
What does all this have to do with English?		
	Daniel: I'll know the words I need to know to answer the questions.	
	Betty: You can put 'tree' [said in English.] in place of arbol. (she is pointing at the white board where Elisa had written some of the sentences students had generated.)	After Betty's comments Elisa asks the students "what can I put in place of..." with each of the Spanish words they had used to describe the picture. The students excitedly call out the English words.
If you know English, can we do sentences in English?		
	Ss: Yes.	
And later can we do paragraphs?		
	Ss: Yes.	
And later can we do essays?	Ss: Yes.	

Elisa carried this message throughout her first day of guided reading: "If you can do it in Spanish, you can do it English." Elisa led the students through a great deal of meta-conversation about language. She told the students that when they are learning a second language, their minds will have to work extra hard, and that sometimes they will have to think first in Spanish to get the job done. Students were eager participants in these conversations and shared stories about bilingual relatives or community members who spoke English and Spanish fluently. In our conversations after the first day of guided reading, Elisa explained that she constructed the activities of the first day this way to make her students feel comfortable with their language abilities.

In this particular reading group, Elisa's presentation of Spanish as a direct way to make sense of English had important consequences in the ways students approached learning tasks. During the group's interaction, the students eagerly explored new ways they would be able to use English. Together with Elisa, the students listed learning goals they would one day achieve. Elisa established a justification for the students' work in the guided reading group that extended beyond obligation. Her framing of learning English created excitement for the students.

This excitement surfaced as the students discussed what they would be able to do with English. Daniel proclaimed he "will know the words that he has to know to respond [to questions]." And, Betty unsolicited offered her English knowledge to the group suggesting Elisa substitute "tree" for the Spanish word "arbol." The instructional context established by Elisa in this first day of guided reading allowed students to develop a meta-understanding of the reasons to learn English. Additionally, the context established by Elisa made it clear to the students that she viewed Spanish as a language learning resource.

A Structure for Letting Kids Show What They Know. During guided English reading there were several examples of student participation that indicated students had opportunities to show what they knew. In the following example, one day after the previous example, Elisa gave each student an English trade book of 15-20 pages. The students read each of their books in overlapping turns. As the students read, Elisa spent one minute listening and helping each student. When the group had finished, she gave each of the students a moment to share the book with the group and explain if they would recommend the book. Unlike her first day of English guided reading, Elisa spoke almost exclusively in English. The following exchange, which occurred as Alma discussed the plot of the book she had read, indicated the nature of student and teacher language usage in English instruction.

Table 13 Elisa Classroom Excerpt: Guided Reading		
Elisa	*Students*	*Action*
OK, Alma can you tell us more about your book?		
	Edgar: I like more this one.	Edgar is pointing to Alma's book but holding his book in his other hand.
(Warmly) In English.	Alma: In English or in Spanish?	
	Alma: This is a story about a tree, the bird shows that that it is his tree, the bee says that it is his tree, the lady bug says it is my tree, this one says it is my tree, this one says it is my tree. [She stumbles a bit on the last two words.]	As she is talking, she is flipping through the pages of the book, pointing at the pictures.
Ok, what is?		
	Lilia: A bee. The girl says this is this is my tree. And the man says is **my** tree and the little girl says is **my** tree, and the little girl says this not this **our** tree.	
What was he trying to do?	Ss: Trying to cut down the tree.	

Table 13 Elisa Classroom Excerpt: Guided Reading		
Elisa	*Students*	*Action*
Do you think that is good?		
Why not?	Ss: (immediately) No. (Students calling out answers) Carlos: Waste.	
It's a waste oofff (laughing)	Gustavo: Time. Carlos: Paper. [overlapping	
Paper, huh, you guys got that down.	Gustavo's turn]	Students have their hands raised and are being called on by Elisa.
(Still sort of laughing) Why do you think that he wants to cut down the tree for?		
For leña, for wood.	Alma: For leña.	
	Carlos: To get wood. Edgar: To make a pencil. Alma: Para hacer mesitas. [To make tables.]	Alma raises her hand and is called on by Elisa.
Right, to make furniture.		
	Edgar: To get wood and make a fire and put fish in there to cook it.	
Yea, he could be getting the wood for fire.	Alma: To make things of wood.	
What do you think is it good to cut down trees?		

Table 13 Elisa Classroom Excerpt: Guided Reading		
Elisa	*Students*	*Action*
No, not even if they are old. So all these animals live in the trees, have you seen any of these animals in the trees? Did you like your book?	Ss: No! Alma: Yea. Gustavo: (Not called on) Teacher, I saw them in the parque [park]. Edgar: I like it more than mine. Alma: Because they show us about trees and valleys. Um, um, they show us that when the autumn comes they fall these leaves and then the leaves they fall and sometimes the leaves don't fall.	Elisa points to pictures of animals in the book. Alma nods and Edgar speaks over her.
Yes, are the leaves falling right now? In April yes, Is it OK to kill ants? No. Thank you we learned some really interesting things.	Edgar: En [in] April, uh uh we go to the mountains and we see saw ants and they smell and we killed them.	

When Elisa transitioned to the next student to summarize his book and said, "Thank you we learned some really interesting things," there was a great deal of sincerity in her voice. Her words of gratitude were representative of her instructional goals that centered around getting the kids to talk. "Me encanta cuando hablan" [I love it when they talk] she said of her students in the Phase 1 interview. For Elisa, student conversation was a valuable part of the student learning process.

In this event, Elisa asked three types of questions, all of which were directed at getting the students to talk. The first type of question was a Narrative Extension Question. As Alma was explaining the plot of her book, she stumbled on the "bee" a second time. Elisa asked, "Ok, what is?" Elisa's question had the effect of extending the student's response. A second type of question was related to a story event, "What was he trying to do?" These types of questions focused students' attention on the story and generated more student talk about events of the story. A third type of question centered around a concept that was partially or peripherally related to the story. In this exchange, Elisa asked the students "Do you think it is good, (to cut down trees). Why not?" This type of question allowed students to participate in a meaningful conversation connected to the texts they were reading.

In addition to offering examples of the types of questions Elisa used in instructional situations, this exchange between Elisa and her students showed knowledge was generated in a multidimensional participant structure situated in meaning-based discussions. Both the students and their teacher generated the elements of English that were the focus of instruction—including new vocabulary words. This process was evident when Elisa asked the class, "Do you think that is good [to cut down trees]?" Although the initial question received only a one word response, she attempted to extend the discussion by saying, "It's a waste of..." Eventually, Elisa rephrased the question completely and a discussion about "leña" [wood] was started by the students. In this context, they were learning new English vocabulary connected to a larger concept-based question posed by their teacher. Students covered a complex range of issues and were eager participants in these conversations.

In addition to this literacy event, there were other examples when in the course of reading books, students posed complex questions and participated in multidirectional discussions. In one example, the class considered if a story with a talking dragon and bear was real or fantasy.

Table 14 Elisa Classroom Excerpt: Complex Questions		
Elisa	*Students*	*Action*
I wonder if, I wonder who lives in the cave? Could a dragon live inside a cave?	Edgar: No Gustavo: Yeah. Alma: In fantasy.	Gustavo has just finished telling the group about his story. In the story, a boy wonders what could be in a cave by his house. He imagines a litany of things: including a bear and a dragon.
In fantasy do they really exist, a bear could be in the cave?	Carlos: Yes Alma: (hand up reporter style and sort of butts in) Teacher, if a dragon is fantasy why in *Japón* do the dragons have good luck and they never (shaking her head) have them.	
In *Japón*, that is a very good question. They believe the dragons are	Carlos: Real.	
That is a very good question—it has to do something with religion. You know what tomorrow we should investigate a book about Japan.	Edgar: (excitedly) Tenemos un libro que dice Japan. [We	

Table 14 Elisa Classroom Excerpt: Complex Questions		
Elisa	*Students*	*Action*
Oh, we have one.	have a book that says Japan.] Alma: No, pero se ven las cities, y cómo le dicen, y (she shakes her head in disappointment) [No, but it only shows the cities and how they are named.]	

In this event, the structure of the interaction proved to be flexible enough to allow Alma to pose an interesting question to the group. Elisa's response to Alma's question revealed her comfort with student-driven instruction. In this event, Elisa continued a student-initiated discussion, which allowed Edgar and Alma to consider and evaluate a potential information source as an answer to the original question.

Guided Reading Makes a Second Shift The preceding literacy events reflect Elisa's energy and commitment to teaching her students. Despite her confusion about how to structure and implement the transition program, she maintained space for her students to be meaningful participants in the process, and she continued to use the language of her students as an instructional resource. In the guided reading events examined, Elisa scaffolded student participation through questioning strategies and her use of Spanish.

Although her commitment to using Spanish as a resource partly guided literacy instruction, Elisa was influenced by a second, competing factor. In early May, Elisa was attempting to find ways to make use of some of the material from the Open Court Transition Review. She was concerned that because Helen had chosen it as the school's transition program, she had to use it. About the same time, she spent some time in the ELD Kindergarten teacher's room. She was shocked to find out that the students of the kindergarten class knew all the sounds on the Open Court Sound-Spelling cards. Watching the kindergarten teacher use the cards with her students made Elisa feel that if her students could master the "sounds" their English reading ability would improve.

Her enthusiasm with the Sound-Spelling cards ran counter to the nature of her instructional orientation in both primary language and English instruction. For the most part, literacy instruction in Elisa's room had a whole-language, meaning-based orientation. Nevertheless, Elisa's desire to be true to the official Transition Review program and her experiences watching the kindergarten teacher caused Elisa to practice the sounds with each guided reading group before they worked on their reading assignments. At this point in the year, the guided reading books were becoming increasingly complex, and most students were reading them well.

The focus on phonetic sounds seemed to be a strange juxtaposition in this classroom that, for the most part, had been focused on meaning. Elisa was quick to embrace the idea that practice with the Sound-Spelling cards would help her students. Her move away from a meaning-based instructional strategy to a focus on decoding English phonemes was related to her uncertainty about the best way to transition her students. For Elisa, the static and highly structured nature of teaching the sounds offered a marked contrast from the instability of developing the transition program. This shift from a meaning-based classroom to a focus on phonetic exactness in reading instruction created different types of student participation than was typical of earlier events, as evidenced by this interaction with a small reading group:

Elisa holds up the Hen card (which is a green vowel card with the letter "e" in red). The three students call out the "h' 'h' 'h.'

Elisa responds, "I always get in trouble with this one. This is a hard. We always get in trouble with this one. I think this is a really hard one. Listen to the sound. (She points the 'e' on the back of the card.) Listen to the sound 'he' hen. That's a hard one will put it on the side." She puts the Hen card on the table.

She pulls out the "hound dog' card and the three girls make the "h" sound.

Table 15 Elisa Classroom Excerpt: Sound Spelling Cards		
Elisa	*Students*	*Action*
(Very excited tone in her voice) I love this one.		Elisa holding the camera card.
	Ss: Kah kah kah	
That's right like a camera. And the "kah" sounds with the C, the K, and the C K at the end right.		
		Elisa grabs the little chalk board. And writes: "k c __ck"
How about a word with the K?		
	Alma: Clock.	
Clock is C, but that is a really good guess. What meows at night?		Elisa writes "clock." As she speaks she points to the "c" and the beginning of the word.
	Betty: Cats	
Yes, but los chiquititos son kittens.		
	Alma: Camera.	Elisa writes kittens on the board.
What did you? (To Alma, points to the card)		
	Oh, clock.	
That is an easy one. What did you say before.		She writes clock.
That one ends with a C and K too, huh.		

During the time Elisa devoted to practicing the sound spelling cards, the level of instructional discourse between teacher and student switched from meaning-based discussion topics to discussions about the sounds of individual letters. Surprisingly, Elisa did not seemed to be bothered by the change in classroom discourse.

Summary of Classroom Events in Elisa's Room

Literacy instruction in Elisa's room was governed by the change and instability exhibited in the guiding reading event. Whether changing the composition of student groups or moving from meaning-based teaching to a phonics-based instructional orientation, change was the name of the game. Although part of the changing nature of instruction was related to Elisa's willingness to tinker until she got things right, part was related to her uncertainty about the best kind of learning environment to create for her students. In this sense, generalizing the nature of literacy instruction in Elisa's room was a very difficult task. At times, the structure of literacy instruction maximized student participation. At other times, English instruction centered on a reductive approach to teaching literacy that dramatically altered the nature of student participation in literacy events.

Local Enactment of Practice and Individual Qualities

The local enactment of policy in Elisa's room shows how the individual qualities of teachers can influence their responses to new policies. In Elisa's classroom, there was no direct correlation between her individual qualities and her literacy practice. Rather, her professional and personal identity interacted with the demands of her teaching situation. Her experience of the new policy context created by Proposition 227 was situated in who she was as a teacher and her role as the school's transition teacher.

In Elisa's case, two individual qualities surfaced as highly significant as potential explanatory factors of practice in Elisa's room. First, her entry into the field of teaching and her reasons for becoming a bilingual teacher; and, second, her perception of her own expertise regarding the task she was officially charged with completing. The local enactment of practice in Elisa's room indicated that the individual qualities of teachers do not influence teachers' reactions to policy changes in a vacuum, but are situated in the larger work context of the school.

Professional Entry and Educational Experience Elisa's classroom practice was in part characterized by structures that allowed her students to be full participants in instructional conversations. During English instruction, she used Spanish as an instructional resource. She made sure her students knew their first language was valued in her classroom. Her reasons for making this explicit to her students were rooted her own educational experience. Elisa had always wanted to work with Latino children because she wanted to give something back to her community. Her reasons for choosing to work in a bilingual school were directly related to her own negative experiences with American schools.

> Tom: I wonder what made you want to be a part of a primary language program? I can see why you would want to work with immigrant Latino students, but why in a bilingual program?

> Elisa: When I was seven years old and got here, I was put in a second-grade class and all through my elementary school I was just passed along. I don't remember anything from school. When I got to sixth, or seventh grade, that's when I started speaking a little bit more English, but my experience from second grade to sixth grade—no me acuedro nada [I don't remember anything].

> So, I started thinking...Porque debería ser asi [Why does it need to be like this]. I was like mucho niños son asi [many children are like this], and I remembered, (she imitates a monotone teacher voice) "This is a car, this is a table, this is the color green, this is red." But, I kept wondering: All of these kids are going through the same thing here. And no debería ser asi [it doesn't need to be like that]. Everything I do in the classroom I explain to the kids why they're going to use it in the future, and how they are going to use it.

Although Elisa was sometimes confused about how to shape her class, she rarely wavered from her claim that "it doesn't need to be like that." Working under the new Charter and in the policy context created by Proposition 227 created instability for her, but Elisa attempted to make her classroom a space in which students would feel more than the unpleasant memories she held of her own education. Her commitment to giving students a space to talk and her treatment of Spanish as a resource in English language development were evidence that her intentional entry into the field of bilingual education and her own educational experience mirrored and influenced the way literacy practice was enacted in her room. Her personal experiences imbued her classroom with a sense of Latino pride.

Perceived Expertise and Instructional Role. Although she felt confident about her ability to create a classroom environment that responded to and addressed some of the deficiencies of her own education, Elisa still felt a great deal of insecurity in her role as the school's transition teacher. Some of her insecurities stemmed from her confusion about how students best learn English. This confusion was partly responsible for her momentary fascination with getting the students to "learn the sounds."

The role that her perceived expertise played in the negotiation of her literacy instruction shows that individual qualities are context-sensitive. Elisa felt quite confident about her abilities to teach students in their primary language, and, consequently, primary language instruction in her classroom did not have the dramatic shifts that characterized English instruction. In addition, the context of her work situation as well as her relationship with her principal created a situation that she felt that there was no one to turn to.

CONCLUSION: TEACHER POSITIONING AND LITERACY INSTRUCTION AT OPEN VALLEY

Like Westway, the local enactment of practice at Open Valley differed between the two teachers in the study. Unlike the teachers at Westway, Angelica and Elisa shared remarkable similarities in terms of their educational histories and their reasons for entering the field of bilingual education. What they shared in individual qualities related to what they shared in negotiating and constructing their classroom practice. Both teachers translated negative personal educational histories into classroom contexts that validated the personal, academic, social, and cultural lives of their students. The role that their individual qualities played in their negotiation of literacy instruction was in some ways parallel to Celia's experience at Westway. All three teachers attempted to create classrooms that addressed shortcomings of their own educational experiences. The ability of the three teachers to achieve those goals was also related to the overall contexts in which they taught. For Celia, the nature of the Open Court Program and the manner in which it was implemented limited her ability to achieve her goals. Angelica, who was not limited by the curricular arrangements at her school, was able to employ a wide range of strategies to create a classroom context that facilitated meaningful student participation.

Although there were similarities in the negotiation of practice for Angelica and Elisa, there were also striking differences. Angelica parlayed her confidence in her own teaching ability and her belief about the benefits of primary language instruction into a local enactment of practice that was always meaning based. She felt little doubt about the decisions she made. Elisa was less sure. In part related to her perceived lack of expertise in the area of second language development, she struggled to create a program she felt would benefit her students. Her struggle eventually led her to spend class time "teaching the sounds." Her fascination with the "the basics" may have been related to the instability surrounding developing and implementing the transition program. Perhaps the static and controlled nature of "teaching the sounds" offered her a break from the challenges of developing and implementing the transition program. Elisa's emphasis on "teaching the sounds" created interactions in her classroom similar to those that occurred in Connie's classroom. While the underlying reasons for the similarities may have been different, Elisa's decision-making process in the classroom highlights the fact that just because a teacher has a certain type of educational experience or ideological orientation, a certain type of pedagogy is not ensured.

CHAPTER 7

Conclusion

Two years after voters all but banished bilingual education, students who speak little or no English scored better on the state's high-stakes standardized test, but the improvement was most dramatic in lower elementary grades and mathematics.

The increases garnered by the one in four California pupils who are still learning English paralleled those of their fluent peers, but the marks mostly hovered in the bottom third nationwide. Their release reignited the debate over whether immigrant children learn best when immersed in English...

Silicon Valley entrepreneur Ron Unz, father of 1998's anti-bilingual education Proposition 227, trumpeted the results as proof that teaching students in English from Day One is best. (*Mercury News*, 2000, August 15)

Several national newspapers including *The New York Times* and *The Los Angeles Times* told similar stories in the days following the release of California's SAT 9 scores. A headline on the front page of *The New York Times* read, "Increase in Test Scores Counters Dire Forecasts of Bilingual Ban" (*The New York Times*, 2000, August 20). Bilingual education has taken a front-and-center position in national discourse. As the excerpt from the *Mercury News* indicates, the examination of the influence of Proposition 227 has focused on rising test scores.

Student performance on the SAT 9, a test considered by many test experts to be an inaccurate and inappropriate measure of culturally and linguistically diverse students' academic achievement (Garcia, 2000), has become the yardstick by which the success of Proposition 227 is being measured.

As high praise for Proposition 227 continues to find its way onto the front pages of our nation's newspapers, researchers, policy-makers, and ultimately the public need to look behind the numbers at the reality of policy change and policy implementation. The headlines touting rising test scores are rooted in the same assumptions that have guided past investigations of policy. The claims behind the headlines are grounded in *input-output models* of policy studies. Proposition 227 changed the way children were educated, the logic follows, and the effects of that change can be measured by standardized tests. Implicit in the current examinations of Proposition 227 is the assumption that teachers dutifully carried out the mandates of the policy initiative in a uniform fashion. Teachers, rarely mentioned in any of the current accounts (The *Los Angeles Times*, 2000, August 15; The *New York Times*, 2000, August 20; *Mercury News*, 2000, August 15), are viewed as the instruments that make the policy happen. In the view portrayed by the media, teachers do the work that allows the policy to be measured using standardized test score data.

The current discussion of Proposition 227 in the news media differs greatly from the analysis presented in this report. Far from being the sole force that shaped the nature of literacy instruction, Proposition 227 was one factor contributing to the context of instruction. Far from being mere conductors of policy, the four teachers of this study negotiated the mandates of Proposition 227 in various ways. They were active participants in determining what the influence of Proposition 227 would be in each of their classrooms. That influence was closely related to who they were as professionals, and their experiences of and reactions to the decision made by their schools and district regarding Proposition 227 implementation.

My research attempts to make the case that the story of Proposition 227 cannot be seen as the "death of bilingual education" and is not accurately reflected in test scores. Policy changes unfold in complex situations. By focusing on teachers' roles in the enactment of policy mandates, my goal was to come to a more accurate understanding of the influence of Proposition 227 on teachers and classroom practice. To this end, I will highlight four major findings of this research. My hope is that these conclusions can be used in a continued investigation into the education of culturally and linguistically diverse students, their teachers, and the policies that affect them. The four major conclusions I will discuss are:

> Understanding the local enactment of policy requires seeing teachers as more than "conductors" of policy.
>
> The individual qualities of teachers play large roles in the translation of policy to classroom practice.
>
> Proposition 227 was not the answer to school and district concerns for English language learners.
>
> Content and instructional practice related to students' lives shapes the nature of student participation in positive ways.

The major findings and conclusions of this report are designed to help teachers, researchers, policy makers, and the voting public better understand the nature of Proposition 227 and its influence on the teachers and students of California. The conclusions presented move beyond seeing the influence of Proposition 227 as merely test scores and programmatic change.

TEACHERS ARE MORE THAN POLICY CONDUCTORS

Many researchers interested in understanding the complexities of classroom practice have focused on teacher beliefs (Clandinin, 1985; Elbaz, 1981; Grossman, 1990; Shulman, 1987). For example, Genishi, Dubetz, & Focarino (1995) considered how teachers' implicit theories about the way students learn have functioned as theories of practice for teachers that underlie teachers' curricular decisions and interactions with their students. While research on teaching has recognized the complexity of teachers' work, traditional educational policy evaluation has viewed teachers as conduits of policy. There is a need to investigate the local enactment of policy in the daily lives of teachers and students, "to look at policy with a pedagogical eye" (Darling-Hammond, 1990, p. 340).

This examination of teachers' work in the new policy context created by Proposition 227 indicated that teachers were not merely conducting the mandates of the law. Many factors—teachers' beliefs about the needs of their students, their ideological orientations to the language and culture of their students, and the structure of Proposition 227 implementation decisions at their schools—contributed to the way teachers experienced the policy context. Teacher action in the new policy context was not a matter of "conducting"; rather, teachers established patterns for professional action through their experiences of the new features of the policy context.

For example, the implementation features of Westway Elementary, which included English Only and Open Court, enabled first-grade teacher Celia to raise issues about the education of her students that had been excluded from school-wide instructional discussions. Although it is difficult to assess what the long-term implications of her efforts will be, her actions in the new policy context indicated that teachers do not just function as passive conduits of policy mandates. Her attempts at exercising agency at the classroom and school level showed that teachers take actions to shape the way policy is experienced.

Similarly, at Open Valley, Angelica, and to a lesser extent Elisa, worked to shape the school's overall response to Proposition 227. During the first year of Proposition 227 implementation, Angelica was very active in securing the parental waivers that allowed the school to maintain its bilingual program. During the second year, she continued her professional action in response to Proposition 227 implementation with her involvement in the development of the Charter and advocacy for bilingual education at the local school level. Angelica took direct action in response to the mandates of Proposition 227 that influenced the nature of the school's implementation of the new law.

By looking at the four teachers in this study, it is apparent that viewing teachers as "conductors" of policy does little to explain the realities of the local enactment of policy. The conductor metaphor connotes a passive transmission. Considering teachers as active participants in the policy process offers a deeper understanding of the way policy influences teachers' work at the local school level. Locating policy studies in the work worlds of teachers offers a clearer perspective on possible explanatory forces that are at work in the enactment policy.

When policy research and policy evaluation merely look at program type and test scores, a great deal can be missed. The classrooms of Connie and Celia were cases in point. Although they worked in the same school, with the same language arts program, their experiences of Proposition 227 were quite different. Those differences not only showed up in their responses to the features of the new policy context, but also translated to their classroom practice. Both teachers' classrooms shifted from classrooms classified as "bilingual" to classrooms classified as "English language development" classrooms. Research using input-output models of policy would categorize them in the same way, regardless of the significant differences between them. This has been the logic behind many of the media articles touting the success of Proposition 227. Such attempts, however, take overly simple perspectives on the ways practice unfolds in instructional situations of the same program type, the ways teachers enact and negotiate instructional practice, and the important instructional realities that exist beyond the explanatory forces of standardized test scores.

INDIVIDUAL QUALITIES OF TEACHERS PLAY A LARGE ROLE IN THE TRANSLATION OF POLICY TO PRACTICE

Proposition 227 attempted to prescribe a uniform solution to the educational issues facing culturally and linguistically diverse students. The local enactment of literacy practice in the four focus classrooms indicates that Proposition 227 was only one explanatory factor in determining the context of instruction in the rooms.

The instructional practices of the four teachers in the study looked very different. Even at the same school, with the same Proposition 227 implementation decisions, and the same program, teachers' negotiation of the literacy curriculum varied greatly. At Westway, literacy practice in the classrooms of Celia and Connie represented divergent responses to the Open Court program and English Only. The structure and nature of literacy practice in both classrooms were largely influenced by the teachers' beliefs about the academic and social needs of the students. Connie believed her students' language and culture was an impediment to their academic success. Her beliefs had their roots in her family's immigration history and her feelings about what it meant "to be an American." The deficit-based teaching and prohibitions against speaking Spanish in her classroom were largely influenced by her belief system. In Celia's case, classroom practice reflected the tensions of her own educational history. Having been isolated and excluded from most classroom events as a child, Celia sought to ensure her students' meaningful participation in classroom events. Her room was characterized by a compassionate stance toward the language needs of her students, but a willingness to give the English Language Development model adopted by her school a chance in the hope it would effect change in the future.

At Open Valley, Angelica and Elisa, two teachers whose personal histories facilitated their deep commitments to primary language, differed in perceptions of their abilities to complete their teaching tasks. For Angelica, there was little doubt she was doing the right thing, the right way. This confidence translated to her teaching practice as she created a context that emphasized meaning-based teaching. For Elisa, confusion regarding structuring and implementing the transition program originated in her own doubts about how students best learn a second language.

The roles the individual qualities of the four teachers played in the enactment of literacy practice indicate that attempts to understand the influence of Proposition 227 must begin with an analysis of teachers. Individual qualities—teacher ideology surrounding language and culture, teacher experience and expertise, teacher personal history—all played roles in the structure and nature of literacy practice.

In the face of policy changes, these teachers attempted to find ways to do what they wanted to do. Their attempts unfolded in complex arrangements. At times they were successful, and at others they were not. For example, Celia's actions at Westway were limited by the control arrangements of Open Court. At Open Valley, Elisa's confusion regarding how to develop and implement an English transition program limited her ability to follow her heart. For Angelica and Connie, the arrangements at their particular schools allowed them to set up classroom environments that mirrored their beliefs about the needs of their students. While teachers may have had varied experiences acting on their desires and beliefs, the image of teachers following their hearts in the changing policy context goes a long way to explain the translation of policy to practice.

This reality has implications for all parties interested in changing instructional practice, including teacher trainers. The experiences of these four teachers with Proposition 227 indicate that changing instructional practice is more than just designing policy or giving teachers new tools to change classroom practice. Policy makers and teacher trainers must create real and legitimate space for the individual qualities of teachers. Because the attitudes and ideologies of the teachers played such a large role in shaping educational practice in the new policy context created by Proposition 227 implementation, teacher training programs must be aware not just of imparting teachers with the technical skills to create successful teaching, but must occupy themselves with the much harder task of dealing with potential teachers' ideologies and belief systems. There has been a long line of researchers who have claimed that teaching students requires creating a legitimate space for their personal histories and culture (Garcia, 1999; Miramontes, Nadeau, & Commins, 1997); there is little reason to believe that training future teachers should be any different.

For policy makers interested in educational change, the roles individual teacher qualities play add yet another factor to negotiate in changing school practice. Scholars have long highlighted how the structure of schools as institutions limited the success of potential reforms (Tyack and Cuban, 1995), but now policy makers must think about who the teachers are, what they believe, and how they see the world. Policy must be directed at both changing practice and addressing the complex roles teachers play in educational change. It must also take into account teachers' attitudes and beliefs, and the complex decision-making structures in which these opinions and beliefs play out. My hope is that these lessons are applied by professionals trained in sound educational theories and used to formulate and articulate well thought out policy initiatives and reforms.

PROPOSITION 227 WAS NOT THE ANSWER TO SCHOOL AND DISTRICT CONCERNS FOR ELL STUDENTS

Proposition 227 was, and is, heralded as the magic bullet to close the achievement gap of linguistically and culturally diverse students in California. Based upon the "success" of Proposition 227, several other states are considering, or have introduced, similar ballot measures. The experience of the four teachers in this study, however, demonstrated that Proposition 227 did little to answer the tough questions they faced: how best to transition students from Spanish to English; how much Spanish to use in instruction; how to improve student reading in the second language; and which strategies work best for English language development?

The complexity of these questions and the complexity of the task of teaching students a second language require substantive discussion and planning for teachers, schools, and districts. Miramontes, et al., (1997) argued that because of the complexity and amount of time needed to develop a second language, second language development must be a school-wide goal with significant coordination. Even in a bilingual program model, language planning is an important part of the process. The allocation of language use by time and the specific roles of first and second language literacy must be decided. In turn, whether first language will be used for literacy instruction, or to teach content as well, must also be decided (Fillmore & Valadez, 1986). Furthermore, teachers must still decide the details of how instruction will be carried out in their own classrooms. In other words, adopting a bilingual program model or an English language development model does not provide a detailed plan of how to implement the instructional program in every classroom, for every teacher and every student.

The nature of literacy instruction at the two schools in this study indicated that implementation of Proposition 227 did little to encourage the kinds of planning, discussion, and coordination necessary for successful second language development programs. At Open Valley, a school whose response to Proposition 227 ran counter to the spirit of the law, the process of securing parental waivers during the first year of implementation and the instability of working in the Charter during the second year redirected resources away from developing answers to the tough questions of second language development. For the transition teacher, Elisa, the new policy context offered little guidance about how to facilitate her students' development of English. Proposition 227 implementation did not create a situation where teachers and administrators dialogued about how best to facilitate student learning. Elisa's attempts to find answers were discouraged by her colleagues, who wanted to maintain a posture that all was fine at Open Valley. Realizing their primary language program was on shaky political ground, her colleagues nervously silenced Elisa at meetings when she attempted to bring up issues of the transition program. Clearly,

Proposition 227 did not create a context in which teachers and administrators could dialogue about how best to facilitate student learning at Open Valley.

At Westway, the principal embraced the notion that no matter what the home languages of the students were, Open Court was a viable educational response to their needs. Her attempts to ensure that the teachers at her school "bought into" the Open Court program worked to remove all serious and substantive talk about second language development from school discourse. The school's response to Proposition 227 created an environment where only Open Court issues were considered as valid topics for discussion. Open Court and English Only, the school's Proposition 227 responses, were treated as recipes for second language development. As the experiences of the students in Connie and Celia's classrooms indicated, Open Court did not always provide students with the resources they needed in their development of English. Often, the reductionist literacy practices Open Court entailed limited meaningful student participation. Although Celia attempted to raise issues related to the educational concerns of her students, the overall feeling at the school was captured by the school's principal when she said, "The California populace has made their decision, they've voted, so we have to do the best we can for the kids." At Westway, like Open Valley, dialogue was stymied by Proposition 277 implementation.

INSTRUCTIONAL PRACTICE RELATED TO THE LIVES OF STUDENTS CREATES MEANINGFUL STUDENT PARTICIPATION

Researchers in the field of second language development have identified several features of effective instruction for culturally and linguistically diverse students. Among them are: (1) some use of native language and culture, (2) a balanced curriculum that incorporates both basic and higher order thinking skills, (3) use of instructional strategies that enhance understanding, and (4) systematic opportunities for student-directed activities, among other characteristics (Fillmore, 1985; Fillmore, 1991; Fillmore & Valadez, 1986; Garcia, 1988). While the purpose of this report was not to evaluate teaching in the policy context created by Proposition 227, it is positive to note that some of the teachers in this study found ways to maintain effective instructional in a political climate that worked to limit such practices. Although not all observed instructional practice exhibited the features of effective instruction—particularly instructional practice heavily influenced by Open Court and English Only—some practice revealed that despite the policy changes, teachers found ways to create sound learning environments for their students. I do not mean to blame teachers for acting in accordance with their school's or district's implementation plans. My intent is to credit teachers' ability to raise the level of their pedagogy even when their profession is under attack.

Angelica's insistence on critical thinking and helping students "see themselves in the stories" they read was a prime example of a teacher's ability to create a classroom environment that met the academic and cultural needs of her students. The nature and structure of literacy instruction in her classroom indicated that student participation in such a context was characterized by meaningful ways of interacting with written texts. Angelica created a learning environment that seemed to be an attack against Proposition 227. For Angelica, the language and culture of her students deserved a prominent place in American education. She structured her classroom to represent those beliefs.

Angelica and Elisa viewed Proposition 227 as an assault on the language and culture of their students. Although Elisa faced some insecurities about her classroom practice, she created an instructional context that made it explicit that she valued her students' language and culture as resources in their learning.

It was not the case at Westway that instructional practice created contexts for meaningful student participation. The over-reliance on back-to-the-basics instruction created classroom contexts that showed a lack of student engagement. For Connie, the process became a self-fulfilling prophecy about her students. Her students' boredom and disengaged behavior in classroom fed her feeling that what they needed was more basic skills. The spiral continued until classroom practice focused exclusively on the component parts of reading and skills worksheets. For Celia, there was a continual struggle to facilitate her students' meaningful participation. At times, she succeeded. At other times, the nature of working with English Only and Open Court worked against her efforts to accomplish this goal.

Final Thoughts

During the two years I spent investigating the influence of Proposition 227 on teachers and students, many people asked me a simple yet profoundly important question: "So, was 227 a good or a bad thing?" When people asked this question, they were not interested in academic conceptions of teacher agency or negotiated instructional practice. They wanted to know if Proposition 227 helped or hurt kids.

As someone who has spent two years looking at this policy, it has been difficult to force myself to find a simple answer to this question. A part of me wants to situate Proposition 227 as the latest manifestation of the dominant American educational ideology of assimilation (Garcia, 1999); another part of me wants to explain that the way we treat our immigrants in educational institutions is not different than the way immigrants are treated in workplace or other social institutions (Valdez, 1998); still another part of me wants to offer critiques of Structured English Immersion; and, finally, a part of me wants to defend bilingual education.

Resisting these more academic responses, I have found that the best answer to this question is a story. I tell the story of Angelica. A teacher so committed to primary language instruction that she was on a constant campaign to make sure the needs of her students were met. I tell the story of her work with second grade students who fit all the profiles of "at risk," but read grade level material with meaning and engagement.

I tell people that this story is not a fairy tale. Bilingual education, like all educational programs, takes work. I tell the story of the struggles of the transition program. I explain that despite its problems, students in that program used their first language as a way to make sense of the second language they were learning.

I tell the story of Celia—Celia who believed that Proposition 227 could work if the "wrong people don't get a hold off it." And, I tell the story of the how the wrong people did get a hold of it, and her struggles to wrestle control back from them. I recall her dismay and anger when she received her SAT 9 scores and only two of her students were even close to being on grade level.

I close my story with Miguel. I explain how Miguel experienced a classroom in which "the basics" in English and not Spanish were viewed as the answer to all of the students' problems. I explain how the idea of back-to-basics and English Only have become the rallying cry for many politicians. Then, I recall how Miguel, while working with a back-to-basics worksheet came to the conclusion that understanding and meaning were secondary to his ability to complete the worksheet and identify the "long O sound" in the sentence "Will Pat go to the store?:

> Miguel: (Reading number 5) (Reads in a flat tone with no questioning intonation.) Will Pat go to the store. (Pauses for a moment) Will Pat **go to** the store. (Flat intonation). Will Pat...Pat go to the store? (An almost raised but unnatural intonation on store). [He raises his head from the text]. That doesn't make any sense. (almost smugly) Don't matter. [He picks up his pencil and writes the words "go" and "store" in the Long O column.]

But it does matter, because the lives of children in the state of California lay in the balance. My goal in telling the story is to help people see that Miguel needs an instructional context in which he can conclude that it does matter. Miguel, and the other students in Walton Unified and throughout the state of California, are more than their SAT 9 scores. They are, in Angelica's words, "going to be our future leaders." I close my story with a simple question originally posed by Angelica, "What kind of children do you want to make?"

Focal Events and Literacy Materials

This Appendix lists the focal events observed for each teacher and a brief description of each activity.

Westway: Celia

<u>Sound Spelling Cards</u> A series of cards breaking down the sound-spelling correspondence of each English phoneme. Each card contained a picture that corresponded with the sound. A rhyme corresponded with each picture. Below the picture was a list of all the English spellings that make that sound. The cards were displayed on the walls of all rooms at Westway.

<u>Dictation</u> This activity functioned as a traditional spelling test in Celia's classroom. Celia read a series of words or short sentences to the students. The words were found in the Open Court teacher's guide. Individually, the students wrote the words in their dictation books. The correct spelling of the words were reviewed with the class.

<u>Blending</u> This activity was described in the Open Court teaching manual as the "heart and soul" of phonics instruction. As Celia wrote the sounds of a word on the board, students said each sound. Then, the

students "blended" the sounds of each phoneme together to "say" the word.

Step-by-Step reading Four page decodable texts focused on single sound/spelling combinations. Students in Celia's room needed substantial support to read these texts. Described in the Open Court teaching manual as an opportunity for students to develop fluency in reading through "reading and rereading."

Reading/Writing Connection These one-page worksheets included skill practice in: copying words, fill in the blank exercises, and identifying particular sounds in words.

Anthology These stories were described in the Open Court teaching manual as giving children "opportunities to use their new-found reading skills with a variety of text types." The reading selections in the anthology were connected to thematic units such as "Trying" and "Being Afraid." During story reading events, Celia read the majority of stories to the children.

Whole Group read-aloud Reading aloud was an official part of the Open Court Program. The teaching manual specified certain trade books to be read with certain units. At times, Celia used these books for read aloud. At other times, Celia used Spanish trade books of her own choosing.

Westway: Connie
Dictation Used daily, dictation was one of the major opportunities for writing in Connie's classroom. The students wrote the words in their dictation books. The correct spellings of the words were reviewed with the class. This activity generally lasted ten to fifteen minutes.

Step-by-Step reading A slightly more advanced version of the same series Celia used. In each story, a particular combination of sounds were practiced. The stories were read together by the whole class. Because the stories were only four pages long, there was little plot or character development. In the second grade curriculum, the step-by-step books were a major component of the program's emphasis on phonics instruction.

Anthology   The reading anthology included literature selections organized in themes. There was considerable variation in terms of the students' ability to read the anthology independently. The selections included fiction, non-fiction, and fantasies. The themes included: Rich and Poor, Fossils, and Kindness.

Phonics Review   These worksheets were generally fill in the blank type activities designed for practice with particular sounds and spellings.

Open Valley: Angelica

Read-aloud   Using popular trade books, Angelica read stories aloud to the students in Spanish. Generally, Angelica lead students through a discussion regarding the problem and solution of the story. This activity occurred nearly every day.

Journal Writing   Students were assigned topics by Angelica and given 20 minutes to write. Journal writing occurred nearly every day.

Cuentomundos Reading Groups   Using the Cuentomundos reading series, students read stories in reading groups. All stories and activities in the Cuentomundos series were in Spanish. Angelica used material from the series to develop activities to use before and after the students read the stories. These included: newspaper articles students wrote about the events of the story, letters to the main characters of the story, mini-research projects using big-books from the series, and pre-reading graphic organizers. These activities were done both in small groups and in the whole class. The selections of the Cuentomundos series included fiction and non-fiction trade books.

Into English   This theme-based ESL program has different material for each grade level. Each unit begins with five lessons that build on concepts and vocabulary used in the rest of the unit. The program utilizes relia, posters, and audiocassette recordings of songs, chants, and poems.

Open Valley: Elisa

Primary language reading Primary language reading activities occurred using the Cuentomundos series and small novels. The students read two full novels both in and out of class work. In addition to reading novels, the class used material from the Cuentomundos series. During Phase 1, Elisa made frequent use of extension activities from the series in class time. During Phase 2, students did work out of the Cuentomundos series as homework. Cuentomundos is a literature-based language arts series.

Centers During Phase 2, Elisa designed centers in which students worked when they were not participating in English guided reading. The students worked on various activities including an English listening center, a writing center, and an independent reading center.

Guided reading Using English trade books, Elisa conducted small reading and discussion groups. Most activities for guided reading were generated by Elisa during or before the lessons. For example, after reading a story in English, Elisa asked the students to write about their favorite part of the story.

Transition and Review This was part of the Open Court program that was officially picked as the curriculum for the school's transition program. The program was based on explicit phonics instruction and designed for use in the beginning of the second grade. The Open Court teacher's manual describes its purpose as helping students who have learned how to read at the end of first grade "regain confidence in their ability to read." The program included Step-by-Step reading books and activities concentrating on building students' knowledge of "letter-sound correspondences."

References

Auerbach, E. (1995). The politics of the ESL classroom: Issues of power in pedagogical choices. In J. Tollefson (Ed.), *Power and inequality in language education.* New York: Cambridge Press. 9-33.

August, D., & Hakuta, K. (1997). *Improving schooling for language minority children: A research agenda.* Washington, D.C.: National Academy Press.

Baker, C. (2001). *Foundations of bilingual education and bilingualism. Clevedon, UK: Multilingual Matters.*

Baker, K. & de Kanter, A. (1983). *Effectiveness of bilingual education: A review of the literature.* Washington, DC: U.S. Department of Education.

Banks, J.A. (1995). Multicultural education: Historical development, dimensions, and practice. In J. A. Banks, & C. A. McGee-Banks (Eds.), *Handbook of research on multicultural education* (pp 3-34). New York: Macmillan.

Becker, H. S. (1998). *Tricks of the trade: How to think about your research while you're doing it.* Chicago: University Press.

Bogdan, R., & Biklen, S. (1992). *Qualitative research for education: An introduction to theory and qualitative methodology.* Needham Heights: Allyn and Bacon.

Clandinin, D. J. (1985). Personal practical knowledge: A study of teachers' classroom images. *Curriculum Inquiry, 15*(4), 361-385.

Cohen, D. K., & Ball, D.L. (1990). Relations Between Policy and Practice: A commentary. *Educational Evaluation and Policy Analysis, 12*(3), 331-338.

Cuban, L. (1993). *How teachers taught: Change and constancy in American classrooms.* New York: Teachers College Press.

Cummins, J. (1996). *Negotiating identities: Education for empowerment in a diverse society.* Ontario, CA: California Association of Bilingual Education.

Cummins, J. (1999). Alternative paradigms in bilingual education research: Does theory have a place. *Educational Researcher, 28* (7), 26-32.

Cummins, J. (2000). *Language, power, and pedagogy: Bilingual children in the crossfire.* Great Britain: Multilingual Matters.

Darling-Hammond, L. (1990). Instructional policy into practice: "The power of the bottom over the top." *Educational Evaluation and Policy Analysis, 12*(3), 339-347.

Darling-Hammond, L. (1993). Reforming the school reform agenda: Developing capacity for school transformation. *Phi Delta Kappan* (June), 753-761.

Deal, T.E. (1985). The symbolism of effective schools. *Elementary School Journal, 85* (5), 601-620.

Diaz, E., Moll. L., & Mehan, H. (1986). Sociocultural resources in instruction: A context specific approach. *Beyond language: Socio-cultural factors in schooling language minority students.* Los Angeles, CA: Evaluation, Dissemination and Assessment Center, CSU-LA.

Dixon, C., Green, J., Yeager, B., Baker, D., & Franquiz, M. (2000). "I used to know that": What happens when reform gets through the classroom door. *The Bilingual Research Journal, 24* (1 & 2), 113-126.

Dyson, A. H. (1993). Negotiating the permeable curriculum: On the interplay between teacher's and children's worlds. Urbana, IL: NCTE.

Elbaz, F. (1981). The teacher's "practical knowledge": Report of a case study. *Curriculum Inquiry, 11*(1), 43-71.

Elmore, R. (1995). Teaching, learning and school organization: Principles of practice and the regularities of schooling. *Educational Administration Quarterly, 31(3),* pp. 355-374.

Emerson, R., Fretz, R., & Shaw, L. (1995). *Writing ethnographic fieldnotes.* Chicago: The University of Chicago Press.

English-learners improve Stanford 9 Exam: Better scores on state test are most evident in mathematics and at lower Elementary grades. (2000, August 15). *The San Jose Mercury News.*

Erickson, F. (1986). Qualitative methods in research on teaching. In M. C. Wittrock (Ed.), *Handbook of research on teaching* (3rd ed., pp. 119-161). New York: Macmillan.

Fillmore, L. W (1985). When does teacher talk work as input? In S. Gass & C. Madden (Eds.), *Input in second language acquisition* . Rowley: Newbury House.

Fillmore, L. W. (1992). Second language learning in children: A model of language learning in social context. In E. Bialstok (Ed.), *Language Processing by Bilingual Children* (pp. 49-69). Cambridge University Press.

Fillmore, L. W., & Valadez, C. (1986). Teaching bilingual learners. In M. C. Wittrock (Ed.), *Handbook of research on teaching* (pp. 648-685). New York: Macmillan.

Franquiz, M., & Reyes, M. (1998). Creating inclusive learning communities through English language arts: From *chanclas* to *canicas.* *Language Arts, 75* (3), 211-220.

Fullan, M. G. (1991). *The New Meaning of Educational Change.* New York: Teachers College Press.

Fullan, M.G., & Hargreaves, A. (1992). *Teacher Development and Educational Change.* London: Falmer Press.

Garcia, E. (1988). Attributes of effective schools for language minority students. *Education and Urban Society, 20*(4), 387-398.

Garcia, E. (1999). *Understanding and meeting the challenge of student cultural diversity.* Boston, MA: Houghton Mifflin.

Garcia, E. (2000, January 31). API test is an injustice to students with limited English. Guest editorial *San Francisco Chronicle*, pp. A 19.

Garcia, E. and Curry-Rodriguez, J. (2000). The education of limited English proficient students in California schools: An assessment of the influence of Proposition 227 on selected districts and schools. *Bilingual Research Journal* 24 (1 & 2), 15-35.

Gandára, P., Maxwell-Jolly, J., García, E., Asato, J., Gutiérrez, K., Stritikus, T., & Curry, J. (2000). *The Initial Impact of Proposition 227 on the Instruction of English Learners.* Santa Barbara, CA: Linguistic Minority Research Institute. Available: uclmrinet.ucsb.edu.

Genishi, C., Dubetz, N., & Focarino, C. (1995). Reconceptualizing theory through practice: Insights from a first-grade teacher and second language theorists. *Advances in Early Education and Day Care, 7*, 123-152.

Glass, G. V., McGaw, B., & Smith, M. L. *Meta-analysis in Social Research.* Sage: Beverly Hills, CA, 1981.

Grossman, P. L. (1990). *The making of a teacher: Teacher knowledge and teacher education.* New York: Teachers College Press.

Groves, M. (2000, August 15). English skills still the key in test scores. *Los Angeles Times*, pp. 1.

Gutiérrez, K., Baquedano-Lopez, P., & Asato, J. (2000). "English for the children": The new literacy of the old world order, language policy and educational reform. *The Bilingual Research Journal, 24* (1 & 2), 87-105.

Hanks, W. F. (1996). *Language and communicative practices.* Boulder, CO: Westview Press.

Hargreaves, A. (1994). Individualism and individuality: Reinterpreting the teacher culture. In J. W. Little & M. W. McLaughlin

(Eds.), *Teachers' work: Individuals, colleagues, and contexts.* (pp. 51-76). New York: Teachers College Press.

Heller, M. (1994). *Crosswords: Language education and ethnicity in French Ontario.* Berlin and New York: Mouton de Gruyter.

Jennings, N. E. (1996). *Interpreting policy in real classrooms.* New York: Teachers College Press.

Kerper-Mora, J. (2000). Policy shifts in language-minority education: A mismatch between politics and pedagogy. *The Educational Forum, 64,* 204-214.

Lau v. Nichols, 414 U.S. 563, 94 S. Ct. 786, 39 L. Ed. 2d1 1974.

Lieberman, A. (1995). *The work of restructuring schools: Building from the ground up.* New York: Teachers College Press.

Lortie, D. (1975). *Schoolteacher: A sociological study.* Chicago: University Press.

Macias, R. (2000). *Summary report of the survey of the states' limited English proficient students and available educational programs and services 1997-1998* Washington, D.C.: National Clearing House for Bilingual Education:

McLaughlin, M. W. (1989). *The RAND change agent study ten years later: Macro perspectives and micro realities.* (Report No. CRC-P89-108). Center for Research on the Context of Secondary School Teaching. (ERIC Document Reproduction Service No. ED 342 085).

McNeil, L. M. (1986). *Contradictions of control: School structure and school knowledge.* New York: Routledge.

Miramontes, O., Nadeau, A., & Commins, N. (1997). *Restructuring schools for linguistic diversity: Linking decision making to effective programs.* New York: Teachers College Press.

Moll, L., C. Amanti, D. Neff and N. Gonzales. (1992) Funds of knowledge for teaching: Using a qualitative approach to connect homes and classrooms. *Theory into Practice, 31*(2), 132-141.

Nias, J., Southworth, G., & Yeomans, R. (1989). *Staff relationships in the primary school: A study of organizational cultures..* New York: Cassell.

Olneck, M. R. (1995). Immigrants and education. In J. A. Banks, & C. A. McGee-Banks (Eds.), *Handbook of research on multicultural education*, (pp 310-327). New York: Macmillan.

Olsen, L. (1997). *Made in America: immigrant students in our public schools.* New York, NY : New Press.

Orellana, M.F., Ek. L. and Hernandez, A. (1999). Bilingual education in an immigrant community: Proposition 227 in California. *International Journal of Bilingual Education and Bilingualism* 2 (2), 114-130.

Osborn, M. & Broadfoot, P. (1992). A lesson in progress? Primary classrooms observed in England and France. *Oxford Review of Education, 18*(1).

Ramirez, D. (1992). Executive summary. *Bilingual Research Journal 16 (1 & 2),* 1-62.

Riccardi, N. (1997). Latino crowd hostile to author of bid to curb bilingual teaching. *Los Angeles Times,* November 9, 1997.

Rosenholtz, S. J. (1989). *Teachers' workplace: The organization of schools.* New York: Teachers College Press.

Rossel, C., & Baker, K. (1996). The effectiveness of bilingual education. *Research in the Teaching of English, 30,* 7-74.

Rowan, B. (1990). Commitment and control: Alternative strategies for the organizational design of schools. In C. B. Cazden (Ed.), *Review of Research in Education* (pp. 353-392). Washington, DC: AERA.

Rumberger, R. & Gandára, P. (2000). The schooling of English learners. In G. Hayward and E. Burr (Eds.), *Conditions of Education 2000.* Berkeley, CA: Policy Analysis for California Education.

Sekhon, N. (1999). A birthright rearticulated: The politics of bilingual education. *The New York University Law Review, 74* (5), 1407-1445.

Schmidt, R. (2000). *Language policy and identity politics in the United States.* Philadelphia: Temple Press.

Sizer, T.R. (1984). *Horace's compromise: The dilemma of the American high school: The first report from a study of American high schools.* Boston: Houghton Mifflin.

Shulman, L. S. (1987). Knowledge and teaching: Foundations of the new reform. *Harvard Educational Review, 57*(1), 313-333.

Spradley, J. P. (1980). *Participant observation.* New York: Holt, Rinehart & Winston.

Suarez-Orozco, M. & Suarez-Orozco, C. (1995). *Transformations: Immigration, family life, and achievement motivation among Latino adolescents.* Stanford, CA: Stanford University Press.

Steinberg, J. (2000, August 20). Increase in test scores counters dire forecasts of bilingual ban. *The New York Times*, p. 1.

Stritikus, T. & Garcia, E. (2000). Education of limited English proficient students in California schools: An assessment of the influence of Proposition 227 on selected teachers and classrooms. *The Bilingual Research Journal, 24* (1 & 2), 75-85.

Stritikus, T. & Manyak, P. (2000). *Creating opportunities for the academic success of linguistically diverse students: What does the research say?* Seattle, WA: Office of the Superintendent of Public Instruction, Washington.

Thomas, W., & Collier, V. (1997). *School effectiveness for language-minority children.* Washington, DC: National Clearinghouse for Bilingual Education.

Tollefson, J. (1995). Language policy, power, and inequality. In J. Tollefson, (Ed). *Power and inequality in language education*, (pp. 1-8). Cambridge: Cambridge University Press.

Tyack, D. & Cuban, L. (1995). *Tinkering toward utopia: A century of public school reform.* Cambridge, MA: Harvard University Press.

Valdes, G. (1998). The world outside and inside schools: Language and immigrant children. *Educational Researcher, 27*(6), 4-18.

Vazquez, O., Pease-Alverez, L., and Shannon, S. (1994). *Pushing boundaries: language and culture in a Mexicano community.* New York: Cambridge University Press.

Vulliamy, G. & Webb, R. (1993). Progressive education and the National Curriculum: findings from a global education research project. *Educational Review 45*(1), 21-41.

Willig, A. (1985). A meta-analysis of selected studies on the effectiveness of bilingual education. *Review of Educational Research, 55*(3), 269-317.

Woods, P. (1994). Adaptation and self-determination in English primary schools. *Oxford Review of Education. 20*(4).

Index